20 School St Westbrook,ME
greentreeministries.net
207-854-TREE

Donate a Bible or book by visiting our Amazon wish list and ship to: 20 School St. Westbrook, Me. 04092

greentreeministries.net/support/

Jesus the Bridegroom

Jesus
the
Bridegroom

*The Greatest Love Story
Ever Told*

BRANT PITRE

IMAGE
New York

Published in the United States by Image, an imprint of the Crown Publishing Group,
a division of Random House LLC, a Penguin Random House Company, New York.
www.crownpublishing.com

IMAGE is a registered trademark and the "I" colophon is a trademark
of Random House LLC.

Library of Congress Cataloging-in-Publication Data
Pitre, Brant.
Jesus the bridegroom: the greatest love story ever told /
Brant Pitre.—First Edition.
1. Jesus Christ—Crucifixion. 2. Messiah—Biblical teaching. 3. Bridegrooms—Miscellanea.
4. Jesus Christ—Jewish interpretations. I. Title.
BT453.P58 2014
232'.3—dc23
2013037088

ISBN 978-0-7704-3545-5
eBook ISBN 978-0-7704-3546-2

Printed in the United States of America

Book design by Helene Berinsky
Jacket art by Bridgeman Art Library

10 9 8 7 6 5 4
First Edition

For my wife, Elizabeth,
and our children,
Morgen, Aidan, Hannah, Marybeth, and Lillia

Psalm 128:3–4

CONTENTS

Your Maker is your husband, the LORD of hosts is his name;
and the Holy One of Israel is your Redeemer,
the God of the whole earth he is called.

—Isaiah 54:5

I am not the Messiah, but I have been sent before him.
He who has the bride is the bridegroom.

—John 3:28–29

This world is the betrothal . . . the wedding will be in the days
of the Messiah.

—*Exodus Rabbah* 15:31

INTRODUCTION

What do you see when you look at a crucifix? Different people see different things. Do you see the brutal execution of an ancient Jewish man at the hands of the Roman authorities? Or the unjust punishment of a great teacher, who was tragically misunderstood by the leaders of his day? Do you see the martyrdom of the Jewish Messiah, who was killed for claiming to be "the king of the Jews"? Or the sacrifice of the divine Son of God, who willingly took upon himself the sins of the world?

In the first century A.D., the apostle Paul—a former disciple of the Jewish rabbi Gamaliel—saw all of these things. But he also saw something more in the crucifixion of Jesus of Nazareth. Paul saw *the love of a bridegroom for his bride.* In one of the most famous (and controversial) passages he ever penned, the apostle describes the passion and death of Jesus in terms of the love of a husband for his wife. Speaking to husbands and wives in the church at Ephesus, Paul writes these words:

> Wives, submit to your husbands, as to the Lord. For the husband is the head of the wife as Christ is the head of the church,

his body, and is himself its Savior. As the church submits to Christ, so let wives also submit in everything to their husbands. Husbands, love your wives, *as Christ loved the church and gave himself up for her, that he might sanctify her, having cleansed her by the washing of water with the word, that he might present the church to himself in splendor, without spot or wrinkle or any such thing, that she might be holy and without blemish.* . . . "For this reason a man shall leave his father and mother and be joined to his wife, and the two shall become one." This is a great mystery, and I mean in reference to Christ and the church. (Ephesians 5:21–27, 32)

Now, I realize that many readers may be thinking: *"Wives do what?!"* Why does Paul tell wives to "submit" to their husbands? And why do husbands apparently get off so easy, with the simple command to "love" their wives? Is Paul some kind of apostolic chauvinist? What in the world does he mean when he says such things?

I promise to get to that later on in the book. Before we can, however, we first need to focus our attention on what lies behind these controversial words: Paul's description of Christ as a bridegroom, the Church as his bride, and the crucifixion of Jesus as the kind of ancient Jewish wedding day on which he "loved" her and "gave himself" for her. Indeed, as we will see later on, when Paul refers to the Church being "washed" and "presented" to Christ, he is describing the ancient Jewish bridal bath and wedding ceremony. From Paul's point of view, the torture and crucifixion of Jesus on Calvary was nothing less than an expression of *spousal love.*

What are we to make of this mysterious analogy? To be sure, most Christians are familiar with the idea that Christ is "the Bridegroom" and the the Church is "the Bride." But what does this really *mean?* And what would ever possess Paul to think of such a comparison? If you had been there at the foot of the bloody cross, with Jesus hanging there dying, is that how *you* would have described what was happening? How could a first-century Jew like Paul, who knew how horribly brutal Roman crucifixions were, have ever compared the execution of Jesus to the marriage between a bridegroom and his bride? Is this just an elegant metaphor? If so, why then does Paul refer to it as a "great mystery" (Greek *mysterion mega*) (Ephesians 5:32)?

As I hope to show in this book, it is precisely *because Paul was Jewish* that he saw the passion of Christ in this way. It is precisely because Paul knew Jewish Scripture and tradition that he was able to see the crucifixion of Jesus of Nazareth as more than just a Roman execution, an unjust martyrdom, or even the sacrifice of the Son of God. Because of his Jewish background, Paul saw the passion and death of Christ as the fulfillment of the God of Israel's eternal plan to wed himself to humankind in an everlasting marital covenant. As we will see in this book, from an ancient Jewish perspective, in its deepest mystery, all of salvation history is in fact a *divine love story* between Creator and creature, between God and Israel, a story that comes to its climax on the bloody wood of a Roman cross.

In order for us to see all of this, however, we will have to go "back in time" to the first century A.D. and take off our modern "eyeglasses" and try to see both the love of God and the passion of Jesus the way the apostle Paul and other ancient Christians saw them—through ancient Jewish eyes. In other words, we will have to go back and reread the accounts of the life, death, and resurrection of Jesus in light of ancient Jewish Scripture and tradition.

When we do this, we will discover that Paul is not the only person who talked this way. In the early stages of Jesus' ministry, John the Baptist—another first-century Jew—refers to Jesus as "the Bridegroom" (John 3:29), even though Jesus has no wife. Later on, in one of his most mysterious parables, Jesus refers to himself as "the bridegroom," and calls his disciples "the sons of the bridechamber" (Mark 2:18–19). Moreover, the very first miracle Jesus performs takes place at a Jewish wedding, when he acts like a bridegroom by miraculously providing wine for the wedding party (John 2:1–11). Most striking of all, the last days of Jesus' life—the Last Supper, the passion, and his crucifixion and death—when examined through the lens of ancient Jewish Scripture and tradition, look mysteriously similar to certain aspects of an ancient Jewish wedding. According to the book of Revelation (written by yet another Jewish Christian), the world itself ends with a wedding: the eternal "marriage supper of the Lamb" and the unveiling of the new Jerusalem as the Bride of Christ (Revelation 19, 21).

In other words, when seen through ancient Jewish eyes, Jesus of Nazareth was more than just a teacher, or a prophet, or even the Messiah; he was *the bridegroom God of Israel come in the flesh.* As the Bridegroom Messiah, his mission was not just to teach the truth, or proclaim the kingdom, but to forgive the sinful bride of God and unite himself to her in an everlasting covenant of love. In the words of the *Catechism of the Catholic Church:*

> The Son of God, by becoming incarnate and giving his life, has united to himself in a certain way all mankind saved by him. . . . The entire Christian life bears the mark of the spousal love of Christ and the Church. (CCC 1612, 1617)

So, if you've ever found yourself puzzled by the words of the apostle Paul, or if you've ever wondered exactly what it means to say that Christ is "the Bridegroom" and the Church is his "bride," or if you've just wanted to understand better who Jesus was and why he was crucified, then I invite you to come along on this journey of discovery.

As we will see, by looking at the love of God and the passion of Christ through the lens of the Bridegroom Messiah, we can transform not only the way we see Jesus and his death, but also how we understand baptism, the Lord's Supper, marriage, virginity, and even the end of the world. While many a man throughout history has jokingly described his wedding day as his funeral, Jesus of Nazareth is the only man who ever solemnly described his funeral as his wedding day. This book explains why, and what it means for who he was, why he lived, and why he died on the cross.

Before we can begin to see Jesus differently, however, we first have to go back to the beginning of the love story, and try to see God differently, through ancient Jewish eyes.

1

The Divine Love Story

In the twenty-first century, it has become quite popular in the secular Western world for people to declare, "I don't believe in God!" However, as one contemporary biblical scholar likes to point out, whenever you hear the words "I don't believe in God," if you really want to know what people mean, it is important to ask the question: *"What God* don't you believe in?"

The reason is that in both ancient and modern times people can use the word "God" to mean very different things. Or, you might also say, there are a host of different "gods" for people to believe or not believe in. For some, God is above all *the Creator,* who exists, and who made the world, but who may (or may not) be very involved in the day-to-day affairs of the billions of individuals who pass through this world. For others, God is a kind of impersonal *Higher Power,* who binds all things together, but who has no face. Think here of the popular image of "the Force" from George Lucas's *Star Wars* films. In this imaginary world, the Force is a kind of deity—holding all of existence together and giving power and life to all things. But it is certainly not a person; you can "use" the Force, but you certainly cannot love the Force. Finally, still others may think of God as the *Invisible Problem-Solver.* This is the popular caricature of theism: God is a powerful person "somewhere out there," who can be called upon in times of disaster, war, strife, and trouble, to intervene in earthly affairs—but only, mind you, when we humans are in over our heads and start to lose control. After things settle down again, it's back to business as usual.

These are just a few examples of the many ways of seeing "God" in the modern world. For our purposes here, what matters most is that none of these ways of seeing God—as a distant watchmaker, as an impersonal force that binds everything together, or as a kind of invisible superhuman hero—is the way a first-century Jew like Jesus of Nazareth would have seen God. From an ancient Jewish perspective, the one true God—"the LORD" or "He Who Is" (Hebrew *YHWH*) (Exodus 3:15)—is not just the Creator. From an ancient Jewish perspective, the God of Israel is also a *Bridegroom,* a divine person whose ultimate desire is to be united to his creatures in an everlasting relationship that is so intimate, so permanent, so sacrificial, and so life-giving that it can only be described as a *marriage* between Creator and creatures, between God and human beings, between YHWH and Israel.

Before we can understand what it would have meant for Jesus and the first Jewish Christians to refer to him as "the Bridegroom," we need to understand why it is that ancient Jews referred to YHWH, the God of Israel, as the divine "Bridegroom." In this chapter we will take a few moments to develop a brief profile of the Bridegroom God of Israel. As we will see, from an ancient Jewish perspective, the God who created the universe is a Bridegroom, and all of human history is a kind of divine love story.

THE BRIDEGROOM GOD OF ISRAEL

First, in order to understand what it would have meant to an ancient Jew to refer to the God of Israel as the divine Bridegroom, it is necessary to grasp how they saw the history of Israel, and, indeed, all of human history. From an ancient Jewish perspective, the history of salvation was centered on the events that took place at Mount Sinai during the exodus from Egypt at the time of Moses. And from an ancient Jewish perspective, the relationship between God and Israel that was established at Mount Sinai was not just a sacred bond revolving around the laws of the Ten Commandments. From the perspective of the biblical prophets, what happened at Mount Sinai was nothing less than a *divine wedding*.

The History of the Covenant at Mount Sinai

Most readers of the Bible are basically familiar with the story of Moses, the exodus from Egypt, and the journey to Mount Sinai. As the book of Exodus tells us, sometime in the late second millennium B.C., the prophet Moses rises up, and, through a series of wonders and plagues, frees the twelve tribes of Israel from slavery in Egypt under an oppressive Pharaoh (see Exodus 1–3). After the celebration of Passover and the overthrow of Pharaoh and his chariots by God during the crossing of the Red Sea (Exodus 14–15), Moses and the twelve tribes eventually travel through the desert of the Arabian Peninsula and arrive at Mount Sinai, where the God of all creation declares that he will appear to them on the mountain. To prepare themselves to meet God in person, the Israelites "wash" in water and abstain from sexual relations (Exodus 19). Then, in a momentous and unforgettable theophany, the Lord of Creation appears atop the mountain in fire and smoke and gives the people of Israel the Ten Commandments (Exodus

20). It is at this point that he enters into a special relationship with them known as a "covenant" (Hebrew *berith*). In the words of Exodus:

> And [Moses] rose early in the morning, and built an altar at the foot of the mountain, and twelve pillars, according to the twelve tribes of Israel. And he sent young men of the people of Israel, who offered burnt offerings and sacrificed peace offerings of oxen to the LORD. And Moses took half of the blood and put it in basins, and half of the blood he threw against the altar. Then he took the book of the covenant, and read it in the hearing of the people; and they said, "All that the LORD has spoken we will do, and we will be obedient." And Moses took the blood and threw it upon the people, and said, *"Behold the blood of the covenant which the LORD has made with you in accordance with all these words."* Then Moses and Aaron, Nadab and Abihu, and seventy of the elders of Israel went up, and they saw the God of Israel.... And he did not lay his hand on the chief men of the people of Israel; they beheld God, and they ate and they drank. (Exodus 24:4–11)

From a biblical perspective, a "covenant" was a *sacred family bond* between persons, establishing between them a permanent and sacred relationship. In the Exodus account of the covenant at Mount Sinai, quoted above, we see exactly this kind of relationship being inaugurated. By accepting the terms of the relationship (the Ten Commandments), and by offering worship to God in the form of blood sacrifice, the twelve tribes of Israel are established in a mysterious and sacred relationship with God. This relationship is established by Moses's act of throwing the blood of the sacrifices on the altar (symbolizing God) and on the elders (representing the people). This action symbolizes that the Creator of the world and the twelve tribes of Israel are now in a "flesh and blood" relationship—that is, they are family. Should there be any doubt about this, notice that once the blood of the covenant sacrifice has been offered, the covenant between God and Israel climaxes in a heavenly banquet, in which Moses and the leaders of Israel manifest this familial relationship with God by doing what families do: eating and drinking together, in his very presence.

The Mystery of the Wedding at Mount Sinai

The book of Exodus gives us this history of the events that it recounts as taking place in the desert some fifteen hundred years before the birth of Christ. But this is not the complete story. To understand how an ancient Jew like Jesus saw the meaning of the covenant at Mount Sinai, not only do we need to read the book of Exodus; we also have to turn to the writings of the prophets, such as Isaiah, Jeremiah, Ezekiel, and Hosea.

When you open the pages of the prophets, you will find something remarkable: they boldly proclaim that behind the *history* of the covenant at Mount Sinai lies a deeper *mystery*. From the prophets' point of view, what happened at Sinai was not just the giving of a set of laws, but the spiritual wedding of God and Israel. From this perspective, the God of Israel is not only the Lord of creation; he is the Bridegroom. Likewise, the twelve tribes of Jacob are not just a people; together they constitute the bride of God. Consider the following passages:

> [Thus says the LORD:] "Therefore behold, I will allure her [Israel], and bring her *into the wilderness*, and speak tenderly to her. . . . *And there she shall answer as in the days of her youth, as at the time when she came out of the land of Egypt.*" (Hosea 2:14, 15)

> The word of the LORD came to me [Jeremiah], saying, "Go
> and proclaim in the hearing of Jerusalem, 'Thus says the LORD,'
> *I remember the devotion of your youth, your love as a bride, how you*
> *followed me in the wilderness, in a land not sown.* Israel was holy to
> the LORD, the first fruits of his harvest." (Jeremiah 2:1–2)

> I passed by you again and looked on you; *you were at the age for*
> *love.* I spread the edge of my cloak over you, and covered your
> nakedness: *I pledged myself to you and entered into a covenant with*
> *you, says the LORD God, and you became mine.* (Ezekiel 16:8,
> NRSV)

Although much could be said about these remarkable prophecies,
for our purposes, three points should suffice. First, notice that the
prophets are all looking back to the time of the exodus: when
Israel came out of Egypt, went into the wilderness, and made a
"covenant" with God at Mount Sinai. In other words, the prophets are retelling the story of Mount Sinai as a divine love story
revolving around the covenant. Second, all three prophets depict
Israel at the time of the exodus as a young bride who is being
wooed by her divine Bridegroom to enter into a marriage with
him. In order to win her hand, God "speaks tenderly to her"—or,
literally, "speaks to her heart"—in order to draw her into a relationship of "devotion" or "steadfast love" (Hebrew *hesed*). Third
and finally, this marital relationship is sealed by means of the covenant: in the words of Ezekiel, it is through the "covenant" (Hebrew *berith*) that the people become the bride of God.

     In other words, from the vantage point of the prophets of Is-
rael, behind all of the visible events surrounding the exodus—the
fire, the mountain, the sacrifices, the smoke—lies the invisible mystery of God's wedding day. Building on the words of
the prophets, later Jewish tradition would teach, in the words of

Rabbi Jose, that *"'The Lord came from Sinai,' to receive Israel as a bridegroom comes forth to meet the bride"* (*Mekilta* on Exodus 19:17).

SIN AS SPIRITUAL ADULTERY

From an ancient Jewish perspective, if we look at the God of Israel as the divine Bridegroom, then this changes not only the way we see the Creator, but also the way we see transgressions against God, which we call "sin." For if the God of Israel is not just a Creator, or a Lawgiver, but the Bridegroom, then *sin is not just the breaking of a rule or a law, but the betrayal of a relationship.*

It is hard to overestimate the significance of this insight for understanding the history of salvation. For, as anyone familiar with Bible knows, it is not very long at all after the wedding ceremony that the newlywed bride, the people of Israel, is caught in the act of spiritual adultery.

The History of the Golden Calf and Israel's Idolatry

According to Jewish Scripture, less than forty days after the making of the covenant at Mount Sinai, without Moses knowing what was going on, the high priest Aaron and the leaders of the twelve tribes abandon their covenant with the God of Israel and begin to offer sacrifice to the golden calf:

> When the people saw that Moses delayed to come down from the mountain, the people gathered themselves together to Aaron, and said to him, "Up, make us gods, who shall go before us...." And Aaron said to them, "Take off the rings of gold which are in the ears of your wives, your sons, and your daughters, and bring them to me." ...And he received the gold at their hand, and fashioned it with a graving tool, and made a

molten calf; and they said, "These are your gods, O Israel, who brought you up out of the land of Egypt!" When Aaron saw this, he built an altar before it; and Aaron made proclamation and said, "Tomorrow shall be a feast to the LORD." *And they rose up early on the morrow, and offered burnt offerings and brought peace offerings; and the people sat down to eat and drink, and rose up to play.* (Exodus 32:1–2, 4–6)

The temptation to commit idolatry might at first seem bizarre to modern-day readers. (I for one have never felt any deep desire to fall down before a cow and adore!) Nevertheless, as biblical scholars point out, the last line of this passage discreetly alludes to the kind of physical excesses and immorality that were part and parcel of ancient pagan worship in the Near East. Such aspects of the pagan cults made them a real temptation for the people of Israel, especially when compared to the spiritual worship and moral strictures required by the God of Israel. The worship of the golden calf at Mount Sinai is but the first in a long history of communal acts of idolatry. According to Jewish Scripture, over and over again, generation after generation, the descendants of Israel fall prey to the worship of the false gods of their pagan neighbors—worship that involves acts of not only religious infidelity but also physical immorality, cultic prostitution, and even human sacrifice (for example, Numbers 25; Judges 2:11–15; 1 Kings 11; 2 Kings 15–17, 24–25). The sin of idolatry is ultimately about offering to some creature or created thing the *love* that is due to *God alone,* not only as Creator, but as the divine Bridegroom.

The Mystery of Israel's Spiritual Adultery

Once again, in order to understand how an ancient Jew like Jesus would have seen the reality of Israel's sin, we cannot just read the history in the Pentateuch and the historical books of the Old Testament. In addition, we need to open up the books of the prophets. From the perspective of the prophets, who saw the covenant between God and Israel as a divine marriage, the worship of other gods was not just a transgression of divine law, but an act of *spiritual adultery*.

Consider the following denunciations of the people of Israel and the city of Jerusalem by the prophets Hosea, Isaiah, Jeremiah, and Ezekiel:

> When the LORD first spoke through Hosea, the LORD said to Hosea: *"Go, take to yourself a wife of harlotry and have children of harlotry, for the land commits great harlotry by forsaking the LORD."* So he went and took Gomer the daughter of Diblaim, and she conceived and bore him a son. (Hosea 1:2–3)

> They have forsaken the LORD, they have despised the Holy One of Israel, they are utterly estranged.... *How the faithful city has become a harlot, she that was full of justice!* Righteousness lodged in her, but now murderers. (Isaiah 1:4, 21)

> "Can a maiden forget her ornaments, or a bride her attire? Yet my people have forgotten me days without number.... *Surely, as a faithless wife leaves her husband, So have you been faithless to me, O house of Israel,"* says the LORD. (Jeremiah 2:32; 3:20)

> [Thus says the LORD:] "But you [Jerusalem] trusted in your beauty, and played the harlot because of your renown, and lavished your harlotries on any passer-by. *You took some of your*

*garments, and made for yourself gaily decked shrines, and on them
played the harlot;* the like has never been, nor ever shall be. *You
also took your fair jewels of my gold and of my silver, which I had given
you, and made for yourself images of men, and with them played the
harlot;* and you took your embroidered garments to cover them,
and set my oil and incense before them. Also my bread which
I gave you—I fed you with fine flour and oil and honey—you
set before them for a pleasing odor, says the LORD God. And
you took your sons and your daughters, whom you had borne
to me, and these you sacrificed to them to be devoured. Were
your harlotries so small a matter that you slaughtered my children and delivered them up as an offering by fire to them?
And in all your abominations and your harlotries you did not
remember the days of your youth. . . ." (Ezekiel 16:15–22)

Three key aspects of these prophetic denunciations are worth
highlighting. For one thing, God's command to Hosea to marry
a prostitute is a kind of prophecy-in-action: Hosea symbolizes
God, while his wife, Gomer, symbolizes Israel. By means of this
sign, God reveals that he knows what it's like to experience spousal infidelity. Indeed, God's own relationship with his people is
(what we call today) a "broken marriage," a covenant relationship
shattered by marital infidelity. Moreover, although Israel's spiritual adultery is made manifest by idolatry, it is not confined to it.
From the viewpoint of the prophets, murder, injustice, iniquity
of all sorts—all of these are acts of spiritual adultery, by which
the people of Israel forsake their divine Husband. Finally, notice the element of marital *betrayal* involved. According to Ezekiel,
through her acts of idolatry not only does Israel abandon God;
she also takes all of the wedding gifts given to her by the Lord
to show her love for *him*—fine garments for the construction of
the Tabernacle, gold and silver for the adornment of the sanctu-

ary, and food and drink for sacrificial offerings—and gives them instead to her other "husbands," to other gods. By means of such sins, she becomes an "adulterous wife, who receives strangers instead of her husband" (Ezekiel 16:32).

In sum, if the inauguration of the covenant at Mount Sinai was in its deepest mystery a spiritual marriage between God and Israel, then the breaking of that covenant by means of sin is spiritual infidelity and betrayal. Once again, later Jewish tradition followed the lead of the prophets in describing Israel's idolatry as the breaking of her marriage vows. In the words of one ancient rabbinic teaching: "*God betrothed Israel unto Himself with the words, 'We will do, and obey.'* . . . When they lost the 'We will do' in making the Golden Calf, Moses said to them, 'You have lost the "We will do," observe then the "We will obey"'" (*Deuteronomy Rabbah* 3:10).

THE NEW COVENANT AND THE FORGIVEN BRIDE

A third key to understanding the ancient Jewish idea of the Bridegroom God of Israel may be the most important of all for grasping the mission and message of Jesus. Although in Jewish Scripture the people of Israel betray their divine Bridegroom in repeated acts of spiritual adultery, *God does not give up on his bride, but promises to one day forgive her sins by establishing a new marriage covenant with her.*

In the books of the prophets, one of the most prominent images of the future age of salvation is this image of marital reconciliation between God and his faithless bride. Over and over again, the prophets speak of a future marriage covenant between God and his estranged wife:

> And there she shall answer as in the days of her youth, as at the time when she came out of the land of Egypt. *"And in that day,*

says the LORD, you will call me, 'My husband,' and no longer will you call me, 'My Baal.' For I will remove the names of the Baals from her mouth, and they shall be mentioned by name no more. *And I will make for you a covenant on that day. . . . And I will betroth you to me for ever; I will betroth you to me in righteousness and in justice, in steadfast love, and in mercy.* I will betroth you to me in faithfulness; and *you shall know the LORD."* (Hosea 2:15–20)

Your Maker is your husband, the LORD of hosts is his name. . . . *For the LORD has called you like a wife forsaken and grieved in spirit, like a wife of youth when she is cast off,* says your God. For a brief moment I forsook you, but with great compassion I will gather you. In overflowing wrath for a moment I hid my face from you, but with everlasting love I will have compassion on you, says the LORD, your Redeemer. . . . *For the mountains may depart and the hills be removed, but my steadfast love shall not depart from you, and my covenant of peace shall not be removed,* says the LORD, who has compassion on you. (Isaiah 54:5–8, 10)

Behold, the days are coming, says the LORD, when I will make *a new covenant* with the house of Israel and the house of Judah, not like the covenant which I made with their fathers when I took them by the hand to bring them out of the land of Egypt, *my covenant which they broke, though I was their husband,* says the LORD. . . . *For I will forgive their iniquity, and I will remember their sin no more.* (Jeremiah 31:31–32, 34)

[Thus says the LORD to Jerusalem:] *"I will remember my covenant with you in the days of your youth, and I will establish with you an everlasting covenant. . . .* I will establish my covenant with you, and you shall know that I am the LORD, that you may remember and be confounded, and never open your mouth again because

of your shame, *when I forgive you all that you have done,*" says the
Lord GOD. (Ezekiel 16:60, 62–63)

Several aspects of these prophecies stand out as important. First,
notice that in every case the new covenant between God and
Israel is a marriage covenant, in which God showers his wife
with the bridal gifts of "steadfast love" (Hebrew *hesed*), "compassion" (Hebrew *rahamim*), and "faithfulness" (Hebrew *'emuna*).
Second, notice that the new covenant is directly tied to the forgiveness of Israel's sins. Although she has broken the relationship God established with her during her youth at the time of
the exodus, God promises that one day he will forgive all that
she has done. In the past, she has treated the pagan gods as her
"lord" (Hebrew *baal*); in the future, she will call the God of Israel her "husband" (Hebrew *'ish*). Finally—and this is extremely
important—in each of these prophecies, salvation is not just
about the forgiveness of sins. From a biblical perspective, salvation is ultimately about *union with God.* The God of Israel is not
a distant deity or an impersonal power, but the Bridegroom who
wants his bride to "know" (Hebrew *yada'*) him intimately, in a
spiritual marriage that is not only faithful and fruitful, but "everlasting" (Hebrew *'olam*).

In short, although there are many ways to describe the biblical
hope for the future age of salvation, one of the most frequent and
unforgettable images in the prophets is that of the new covenant
between the Bridegroom God of Israel and his estranged spouse.
From this point of view, all of human history is a story of divine love—given, betrayed, forgiven, and renewed because of the
mercy and compassion of God. In fact, the very prophecies from
Jewish Scripture that we cited above eventually fueled the hope
of the ancient Jewish people for the future wedding of God. In
the words of one ancient Jewish text:

This world is like the betrothal, for it says: "And I will betroth you to Me in faithfulness" [Hosea 2:20]. *The actual marriage ceremony will take place in the days of the Messiah,* as it says: "For thy Maker is thy husband" [Isaiah 54:5]. (*Exodus Rabbah* 15:31)

THE SONG OF SONGS

Before bringing this chapter to a close, there is one final aspect of ancient Jewish beliefs about the Bridegroom God of Israel that demands our attention. In addition to the explicit prophecies of the new marriage covenant between YHWH and Israel, ancient Jewish interpreters also read the Song of Songs as a symbolic description of the future wedding between the Bridegroom God and his chosen people. No study of Jesus the Bridegroom would be complete without a brief look at how this traditional Jewish interpretation of the Song of Songs fed into the hope for the new wedding covenant.

There are, as one might expect, many different ways to interpret the Song of Songs. In modern times it has become very popular to interpret it strictly as a *poem about human love.* From this point of view, the bridegroom is a husband, and the bride is his spouse, and the focus of the poem is on the passionate love of a man and a woman. In the Christian tradition many mystical commentaries have been written on the Song of Songs, which tend to interpret it as *an allegory of the soul.* From this point of view, the bridegroom is God, the bride is the soul, and the focus of the poem is the spiritual union between God and the individual. Last, and most important for our purposes, in ancient Jewish tradition, as far back as we can tell, the Song of Songs was not interpreted as a love poem or as an allegory of the individual soul; it was interpreted as *an allegory of God's spousal love for the people of Israel.*

Indeed, already in the first century, Josephus groups the Song of Songs among those books containing "hymns to God" (*Against Apion* 1:40), and the extra-biblical work known as *4 Ezra* uses images from the Song of Songs to describe the relationship between God and the city of Jerusalem (*4 Ezra* 5:23–28). However, by far the most famous explicit affirmation of a symbolic interpretation is from Rabbi Akiba (ca. A.D. 50–135), who in two of his most famous sayings not only denounces an erotic interpretation of the Song of Songs but also proclaims the Song of Songs to be the holiest book in the Jewish Bible:

> He who sings the Song of Songs in a banquet hall and makes it into a kind of ditty has no place in the world to come. (Tosefta, *Sanhedrin* 12:10)

> All the ages are not worth the day on which the Song of Songs was given to Israel; *for all the Writings are holy, but the Song of Songs is the Holy of Holies*. (Mishnah *Yadayim* 3:4)

In other words, from the perspective of Rabbi Akiba, anyone who treats the Song of Songs as if it is just another popular "love song" is gravely mistaken. Far from being the most profane book in the Bible, the Song of Songs is the most holy, because it is really about the spousal love of God. For Rabbi Akiba, the Bridegroom in the Song of Songs is "He who spoke and the world came to be," and the bride is "Israel" (*Mekilta de Rabbi Ishmael* 3:49–63). Although not every Jew living in ancient times might have agreed with Rabbi Akiba's judgment, all of the ancient Jewish evidence we possess points to the interpretation of the Song of Songs as an allegory of the Bridegroom God and his covenant with Israel. There is no competing view that has lived to see the light of day.

Although an entire book could be written on the Song of Songs, for our purposes we simply want to take a few moments to try to see a few of its passages through ancient Jewish eyes. I do not have the space here to defend the traditional Jewish reading; instead, I simply want to try to help modern-day readers to see how the Song of Songs played into the ancient Jewish concept of the Bridegroom God of Israel so that we can put the hope for the new wedding covenant in its proper historical context.

The Song of Songs and God the Bridegroom

Why would ancient Jewish tradition have identified the bridegroom in the Song of Songs as God? At first glance, the identity of the bridegroom seems clear: he is King Solomon, and the poem is an ode to his wedding day (see Song 3:7–11).

On closer inspection, however, we notice something remarkable: much of the language used to describe the bridegroom in the Song of Songs is used elsewhere in Jewish Scripture to describe the God of Israel. Although these parallels are admittedly easier to see in the original Hebrew, they are striking enough that even in English they can be summarized in the form of a chart:

The God of Israel	The Bridegroom in the Song of Songs
"Hear, O Israel . . . *you shall love the LORD your God* with all your heart, and *with all your soul,* and with all your might." (Deuteronomy 6:4–5)	*Him whom my soul loves . . .* (Song of Songs 1:7, 3:1, 2, 3, 4)
This is the day which the LORD has made; *let us rejoice* and be glad *in it!* (Psalm 118:24)	The king has brought me into his chambers. *We will exult* and *rejoice in you.* (Song of Songs 1:4)

The LORD is my shepherd, I shall not want; he makes me lie down in green pastures. . . .
(Psalm 23:1–2)

Tell me . . . where you pasture your flock, where you make it lie down. . . .
(Song of Songs 1:7)

More to be desired are they [the ordinances of the Lord] than gold; sweeter also than honey and drippings of the honeycomb.
(Psalm 19:9–10)

His speech is most sweet, and he is altogether desirable. . . .
(Song of Songs 5:16)

"'I will take you for my people, and I will be your God.'"
(Exodus 6:7; cf. Leviticus 26:12)

I am my beloved's and my beloved is mine.
(Song of Songs 6:3)

These are just a few of the remarkable parallels between the figure of the bridegroom in the Song of Songs and descriptions of God in the Jewish Scriptures (many others could be listed). Significantly, the shared words and images come from some of the most popular and well-known parts of the Jewish Bible: the book of Exodus, the passage from Deuteronomy 6 known as the Shema', which was prayed three times a day by ancient Jews, Psalm 23 ("The Lord is my Shepherd"), and Psalm 118, which was sung by ancient Jews at major Jewish festivals.

According to Old Testament scholar Ellen Davis, these kinds of Hebrew parallels with other biblical passages about God led ancient Jewish readers to identify the Bridegroom in the Song with YHWH, the God of Israel. As she writes: "The Song of Songs is, in a sense, the most biblical of books. . . . [It] is thick with words and images drawn from earlier books. By means of this 'recycled' language, the poet places this love song firmly in the context of God's passionate and troubled relationship with humanity (or, more particularly, with Israel), which is the story the rest of the Bible tells." In light of such parallels, Davis makes a powerful case that "at one level of the poet's meaning, the one who is loved and sought after so intently is *God*. The poet's original hearers would make this association . . . more easily than we do, because they were familiar with biblical idiom."

The Song of Songs and Israel as the Bride

In support of this explanation, we can turn to the even more elaborate and striking descriptions of the bride in the Song of Songs. Once again, at first glance, the identity of the bride in the Song of Songs seems clear: she is the "Shulammite" woman, the bride of King Solomon, on his wedding day (Song 6:13).

On the other hand, many of the descriptions of the bride in the Song of Songs are, well, *odd*. Her hair is "like a flock of goats, moving down the slopes of Gilead" (Song 4:1). Her teeth are "like a flock of shorn ewes that have come up from the washing, all of which bear twins" (Song 4:2). Her "neck" is "like the tower of David, built for an arsenal . . ." (Song 4:4). This is not the kind of thing a man says to his bride if he wants to compliment her! Indeed, when reading the Song of Songs, it is often difficult to tell whether what is being described is the body of a woman or a building, or a land, or a temple.

One could chalk all of this up to ancient imagery and poor taste. However, when you compare these otherwise bizarre descriptions of the bride in the Song of Songs with the rest of Jewish Scripture, once again, you find that the Hebrew language and imagery used to describe her is also used elsewhere in the Jewish Bible to describe *the Temple and the city of Jerusalem*. Once again, for the sake of space and time, I'll simply chart out a few of these parallels:

The Temple in Jerusalem	*The Bride in the Song of Songs*
And [Solomon] made the [curtain in the Temple] of blue and purple and crimson fabrics and fine linen, and worked cherubim on it. (2 Chronicles 3:14)	I am very dark, but lovely, O daughters of Jerusalem, like the tents of Kedar, *like the curtains of Solomon.* (Song of Songs 1:5)
[Solomon] built the house of the Forest of Lebanon; . . . upon three rows of *cedar* pillars, with *cedar* beams upon the pillars. (1 Kings 7:2)	The scent of your garments is *like the scent of Lebanon.* (Song of Songs 4:11)
In front of the house [Solomon] made . . . chains like a necklace and put them on the tops of the pillars; and *he made a hundred pomegranates and put them on the chains.* (2 Chronicles 3:15–16)	Your shoots are *an orchard of pomegranates* with all choicest fruits. (Song of Songs 4:13)
"On that day there shall be *a fountain* opened for . . . the inhabitants of *Jerusalem.* . . . On that day *living waters* shall flow out from *Jerusalem.* . . ." (Zechariah 13:1, 14:8)	A garden locked is my sister, *my bride.* . . . a garden *fountain*, a well of *living water* . . . (Song of Songs 4:12, 15)

Perhaps most striking of all, at one point, the writer of the Song of Songs comes right out and declares of the bride:

> You are beautiful as Tirzah, my love,
> lovely as Jerusalem.
> (Song of Songs 6:4)

Why in the world would anyone want to compliment a woman by comparing her to an entire city, much less two? (Imagine someone today saying to his fiancée, "You're as big as the city of New York"!) Because, as any first-century Jew would have known, Tirzah was the first capital of the northern kingdom of Israel, while Jerusalem was the capital of the southern kingdom of Judah (1 Kings 15:33; 2 Samuel 5:5). In other words, like the Temple itself, the beautiful bride of the Song of Songs encompasses all twelve tribes of Israel in herself.

More parallels between the Temple in Jerusalem and the bride in the Song of Songs could be given. For now, these should suffice to help us understand how ancient Jews may have been spurred on by the imagery in the poem to interpret it as more than just a love poem about Solomon and the Shullamite woman. In the figure of the bride—whose body resembles the land of Israel and whose appearance and fragrances resemble the Temple in Jerusalem—we may find one reason ancient Jewish interpreters chose to read the poem as an allegory of Israel's love for the Bridegroom God. In the words of Ellen Davis: "The image of the bride . . . is like one of those pictures whose contents shifts before your eyes. . . . Looking closely, we see at one moment a human love scene. . . . Then we blink, and now we see the special intimacy between God and Israel, which reaches its high point in Temple worship."

The Ancient Jewish Hope for the Wedding of God and Israel

With all of this in mind, we can bring this chapter to a close by pointing out that although the Song of Songs is sometimes described as a love poem or wedding song, in fact the poem never actually describes the consummation of the marriage. Instead, the bride spends most of the poem trying to find the bridegroom, who keeps on disappearing (see Song 5:2–8). Although the bride dreams of her future wedding—as young brides tend to do—when the book ends, she is still too young to be married

(Song 8:1–10), and, as a result, her last words are a cry for the bridegroom to come quickly:

> Make haste, my beloved, and be like a gazelle
> or a young stag upon the mountains of spices.
>
> (Song of Songs 8:14)

If we follow the lead of ancient Jewish tradition and see the bridegroom in the Song of Songs as God, and the bride as the people of Jerusalem, then the Song of Songs does not end with a wedding, but with the bride (Israel) waiting for the bridegroom (God) to come. This is exactly how the ancient Jewish Targum on the Song of Songs interprets the bride's cry for the bridegroom to "make haste":

> At the time of our distress, when we pray before You [God], be like a gazelle . . . watch over us and observe our trouble and affliction from the highest heavens, till such time as You are pleased with us and redeem us and bring us up the mountains of Jerusalem, where the priests will offer up before you incense of spices. (*Targum of Canticles* on 8:14)

Notice that in this Jewish tradition, the wedding of God and Israel is consummated through sacrifice and worship. This connection between the wedding of God and worship will be very important to keep in mind over the course of our study. As we will see, Jesus himself will unite mankind to God through an act of sacrificial worship. For now, we simply want to highlight that this is where the Jewish people are at the time of Jesus: they are not just waiting for the kingdom of God, or the coming of the Messiah, or the restoration of the twelve tribes. Above all, they are waiting for the coming of the Bridegroom God of Israel, who will forgive their sins and unite himself to them in an everlasting marriage covenant.

2

Jesus the Bridegroom

Who was Jesus of Nazareth? Why did he live? And why did he die?

Over the centuries, there have been dozens, if not hundreds, of different answers to these questions. Some say Jesus was a great teacher, a Jewish rabbi who lived to tell others about the love of God, and who died because some people didn't like what he was teaching. Others say that Jesus was a great prophet, who lived to proclaim the coming of the kingdom of God, and who died because some people didn't understand that his kingdom was not of this world. Others say that Jesus was the Messiah, who had come to fulfill the prophecies of the anointed king of Israel, and who was killed because the Romans saw him as a threat to their empire. Still others profess that Jesus was the divine Son of God, who became man so that he might offer himself as a sacrifice for the sins of the world.

All of these answers can be found in the pages of the New Testament. But there is one other answer to the question of Jesus' identity that was given long ago, by one of Jesus' most prominent Jewish contemporaries: John the Baptist. On one occasion, when asked what he thought about Jesus' growing popularity, John replies by saying:

> "I am not the Messiah, but I have been sent before him. *He who has the bride is the bridegroom.*" (John 3:28–29)

What is the meaning of this mysterious response? How can John refer to Jesus as "the bridegroom" when Jesus was an unmarried man? What meaning would John's words have had in a first-century Jewish context?

The answer, I suggest, can be found by taking what we learned in the last chapter about God the Bridegroom and Israel the bride and using it to see the words and deeds of Jesus through ancient Jewish eyes. When we do this, all of a sudden we begin to realize that some of Jesus' actions are meant to signal that he is not only the Jewish Messiah; he is *the divine Bridegroom come in person, to fulfill the prophecies of a new marriage covenant.* In this regard, two episodes in the life of Jesus stand out in particular: the miracle of the wedding at Cana at the beginning of his public ministry, and the Last Supper with the twelve disciples at the end. When Jesus' words and deeds at each of these key moments are interpreted in their Jewish context, we begin to realize that these events are more than just a startling miracle or a farewell meal. Rather, they are like bookends, showing that Jesus has come to bring the miraculous wine of the wedding banquet of God and his bride.

THE RIDDLE OF JOHN THE BAPTIST

In order to see this, we need to go back to John the Baptist's riddle-like identification of Jesus as "the bridegroom" and look at it a bit more carefully.

In the early days of Jesus' ministry, when he was just beginning to gather his own band of followers (John 1:29–51), John's disciples approach their master to ask him what he thought about this Jesus and the fact that he and his followers were also baptizing people and becoming so popular (see John 3:26). In response to his disciples' question, John the Baptist answers in this way:

> "You yourselves bear me witness, that I said, I am not the Messiah, but I am the one who has been sent before him. *He who has the bride is the bridegroom. The friend of the bridegroom, who stands and hears him, rejoices with joy because of the voice of the bridegroom.* Therefore this joy of mine is now fulfilled. He must increase, but I must decrease." (John 3:28–30)

For a long time, when I read over these words, they didn't mean all that much to me. Growing up Christian, I was familiar with the idea that Jesus is the Bridegroom and the Church is his bride, so I simply read that into the text: "Christ is the Bridegroom." Check. John the Baptist is just the "best man"—that is, the "friend of the bridegroom." Check. And then I just moved on to the next part of the Gospel. I never really stopped to ask myself the question: What would John's original Jewish disciples themselves have thought he was saying, and what did he expect them to take from his words?

Think about it for a minute: If John really wanted to identify Jesus as the Messiah, then saying "Look for the guy with the bride" is not a very helpful way to do it! For one thing, wasn't the Jewish Messiah supposed to be a king, or a warrior, or a priest? Where does John get the idea that he is a "bridegroom"? Even more to the point: despite the claims of certain recent novels to the contrary, there is no evidence whatsoever that Jesus himself was ever married, and very good reason to conclude that he embraced a life of celibacy "for the sake of the kingdom of heaven" (see Matthew 19:10–12). If Jesus was unmarried, then who is this "bride" that John is talking about? And how does John expect his disciples to be able to identify Jesus as the bridegroom given that he appears to have no wife?

As we will see over and over again throughout this book, the key to unlocking the deeper meaning of many of these familiar passages in the Gospels can be found by trying to understand them in their original, first-century Jewish context. Remember: Jesus was a Jew. John the Baptist was a Jew. For that matter, all of John's disciples and all of Jesus' disciples were also Jewish. There-fore, as a general rule, whenever you find something puzzling or strange in the Gospels—like John the Baptist referring to Jesus as "the bridegroom" even though he is celibate—the explanation is almost invariably to be found by going back to the *Jewish Scriptures.* It is these Scriptures, commonly known in Christian circles as the Old Testament, that will be our primary source for unlock-ing the meaning of the words and deeds of Jesus in the Gospels. However, from time to time, we will also have recourse to *ancient Jewish tradition,* which is enshrined in a number of Jewish writings outside the Bible, such as the works of Josephus, the Dead Sea Scrolls, and the collection of early rabbinic traditions know as the Mishnah. (For a full list of key Jewish sources outside the Bible that we will be drawing on, see the Appendix.) When we look at John the Baptist's "riddle" of Jesus the Bridegroom in the light of Jewish Scripture and tradition, a number of otherwise blurry points start to come into focus.

The Voice of the Bridegroom Messiah

First, when John says he rejoices to hear "the voice of the bride-groom" (John 3:29), this is not just an eloquent metaphor. Instead, it is an allusion to a famous biblical prophecy of *the Messiah*—the "anointed one" (Hebrew *mashiah*), the king of Israel, for whom the Jewish people had been waiting for centuries. In one of the passages from the book of Jeremiah, the prophet connects the hearing of the voice of the bridegroom and bride with the coming of the future Davidic king:

> "Thus says the LORD: In this place of which you say, 'It is a waste without man or beast,' in the cities of Judah and the streets of Jerusalem that are desolate ... *there shall be heard again the voice of mirth and the voice of joy, the voice of the bridegroom and the voice of the bride,* the voices of those who sing, as they bring thank offerings to the house of the LORD. . . . Behold, the days are coming, says the LORD when I will fulfill the promise I made to the house of Israel and to the house of Judah. *In those days and at that time I will cause a righteous Branch to spring forth for David;* and he shall execute justice and righteousness in the land. In those days Judah will be saved and Jerusalem will dwell securely. . . . For thus says the LORD: David shall never lack a man to sit on the throne of the house of Israel. . . ." (Jeremiah 33:10–11, 14–17)

Although they are sometimes overlooked by modern readers, the parallels between this prophecy and the words of John the Baptist are striking. Just as Jeremiah says that "the voice of the bridegroom" will be heard in the days when the Davidic king will come, so too John the Baptist says that he rejoices that he gets to hear "the voice of the bridegroom"—meaning the Messiah. And just as Jeremiah speaks about "the voice of the bride," so too John says that you can know who the Messiah is because he has "the bride." Finally, just as Jeremiah talks about the "joy" of the days when the king will come, so too John the Baptist speaks of his own personal "joy" at having heard the voice of the Bridegroom Messiah.

John Is the Jewish "Best Man"

Should there be any doubt about this, notice how John identifies himself: as "the friend of the bridegroom" (John 3:29).

This is a great example of how we need to look at Jewish Scripture in order to understand the Gospels, but we also need to familiarize ourselves with ancient Jewish tradition. For although the Jewish Bible never uses the expression "friend of the bridegroom," the ancient Jewish rabbis whose traditions are recorded in the Mishnah do use this expression. They refer to the custom of a Jewish bridegroom selecting a close "friend" of his to act as his "best man" (Hebrew *shoshbin*) (see Mishnah, *Sanhedrin* 3:5). According to rabbinic tradition, when the time for the wedding arrived, it was the friend of the bridegroom, the *shoshbin,* who acted as public witness to the wedding, in much the same way that the best man and maid of honor do in contemporary weddings (see *Deuteronomy Rabbah* 3:16).

Indeed, the role of "best man" was so essential to an ancient Jewish wedding that according to Jewish tradition, God himself acted as best man at the wedding of Adam and Eve, since there was no one else to fill the role!

> "And he brought her to the man." (Genesis 2:22). Rabbi Jeremiah ben Elezar said: "This teaches that [God] acted as best man (Hebrew *shoshbin*) to Adam." (Babylonian Talmud, *Berakoth* 61a)

Notice an important insight that this Jewish tradition gives us into John the Baptist's words. According to the rabbis, it was the job of the Jewish best man to bring the bride to the bridegroom when the time for the wedding came. Along the same lines, like any Jewish *shoshbin,* John the Baptist's job is not to be the center of attention. John's task is *to lead the bride to the bridegroom when the time for the wedding has come.* And how does he do this? By calling all of the people of Israel to repentance in preparation for the coming of the Messiah:

> John the baptizer appeared in the wilderness, preaching a baptism of repentance for the forgiveness of sins. *And there went out to him all the country of Judea, and all the people of Jerusalem; and they were baptized by him in the river Jordan, confessing their sins.* (Mark 1:4–5; cf. Matt 3:5; Luke 3:2–3)

As we will see in the next chapter, the act of ritual washing with water was a very important part of a Jewish bride's preparation for her wedding in ancient times. For now, however, we simply want to note that if Jesus is the bridegroom and John the Baptist is his best man, then John is performing his duties according to Jewish custom. By means of his baptism, John is preparing the people of Israel—from all "Judea" and "Jerusalem"—for the coming of the divine wedding through which their sins will be forgiven. And by identifying Jesus as "the bridegroom" and the Messiah, John is also leading the bride, the people of Israel, to her bridegroom. Just as a best man recedes from view at any wedding celebration, so too John the Baptist must recede from view now that the bridegroom is coming. As he says: "He must increase, but I must decrease" (John 3:30).

In other words, when we look at the riddle of John the Baptist in the light of Jewish Scripture and tradition, its meaning becomes quite clear. By means of this riddle, John is saying, in a very Jewish way: "I've already told you: I'm not the Messiah. If you want to know who the Messiah is, *look for the one with the bride.* I'm just the best man."

But this is not the only clue to Jesus' identity as the bridegroom. Even more significant are the words and deeds of Jesus himself, beginning with his first miracle, performed at a Jewish wedding.

THE WEDDING AT CANA

In theory, Jesus could have begun his public ministry in any number of ways. If he had wanted to establish his credentials as a teacher, the first thing he could have done was to preach the Sermon on the Mount. If he had wanted to emphasize his power over demons, then the first thing he might have done was to perform an exorcism in the sight of all, such as casting out the "Legion" of evil spirits living within the Gerasene demoniac. If Jesus had wanted more than anything else to reveal his power over death, the obvious way to begin his ministry would have been to bring someone back from the dead, as in the raising of Lazarus.

As it turns out, however, Jesus did none of these things. According to the Gospel of John, the first public miracle (or "sign") Jesus performed, which set the stage for the rest of his ministry, was *to transform water into wine at a Jewish wedding*. Why? Surely something more momentous would have been more appropriate. Nevertheless, before Jesus displayed his wisdom as a teacher, before he exercised his authority as an exorcist, and before he manifested his power as a healer, the first thing he did was perform a miracle in which he, though unmarried, deliberately acted like a Jewish bridegroom by providing wine for a wedding.

The First of Jesus' Miracles

In order to see this clearly, we need to look carefully at the famous account of Jesus' words and deeds at the wedding at Cana:

> On the third day there was a wedding at Cana in Galilee, and the mother of Jesus was there; Jesus also was invited to the wedding, with his disciples. When the wine failed, the mother of Jesus said to him, "They have no wine." And Jesus said to her,

"What is that to you and to me, Woman? My hour has not yet come." His mother said to the servants, "Do whatever he tells you." Now six stone jars were standing there, for the Jewish rites of purification, each holding twenty or thirty gallons. Jesus said to them, "Fill the jars with water." And they filled them up to the brim. He said to them, "Now draw some out, and take it to the steward of the feast." So they took it. When the steward of the feast tasted the water now become wine, and did not know where it came from (though the servants who had drawn the water knew), the steward of the feast called the bridegroom and said to him, "Every man serves the good wine first; and when men have drunk freely, then the poor wine; but you have kept the good wine until now." This, the first of his signs, Jesus did at Cana in Galilee, and manifested his glory; and his disciples believed in him. (John 2:1–11)

Although this story is well known, it immediately raises a number of puzzling questions. First, why does Mary bring the lack of wine to Jesus' attention? Given the fact that he is clearly a guest at this wedding, it seems strange that she would turn to him with the problem, rather than take it to the host. Second, and even more puzzling, why does Jesus respond to his mother in the way that he does? At first glance, Jesus' addressing Mary as "Woman" comes off as disrespectful, if not downright rude. (I know I could never address *my* mother as "Woman" without serious repercussions!) Moreover, his declaration that his "hour" has not yet come is, to say the least, a strange way to react to Mary's observation that the wine has run out. All she says is "They have no wine." What has that got to do with Jesus' "hour"? Third and finally, and most puzzling of all, given his apparent resistance to Mary's words, why does Jesus then turn around and solve the problem of the lack of wine by performing a miracle?

Clearly, the sign had some meaning to Jesus' Jewish disciples. What was it?

When we explore each of these questions in light of ancient Jewish Scripture and tradition, several key points emerge, suggesting that there is much more going on than at first meets the eye.

Is Jesus Disrespecting His Mother?

The first thing that needs to be said here is that Jesus is not being disrespectful to Mary when he says: "What is that to you and to me, Woman? My hour has not yet come." Although Jesus' response certainly *sounds* disrespectful to our ears, in the language and context of the time it really isn't.

For one thing, Jesus uses "Woman" (Greek *gynai*) on several occasions to address other women—the Samaritan woman, Mary Magdalene, the Canaanite woman, and the woman who was bent over for eighteen years—without any hint of rebuke or disrespect (see John 4:21; 20:13–15; Matthew 15:28; Luke 13:12). Most important of all, he uses the same form of address in the midst of his crucifixion, while he is hanging on the cross:

> When Jesus saw his mother, and the disciple whom he loved standing near, he said to his mother, "*Woman,* behold your son!" Then he said to the disciple, "Behold, your mother!" And from that hour the disciple took her to his own home. (John 19:26–27)

It should go without saying that it would be absurd to suggest that Jesus is being disrespectful to Mary in his final moments before dying. For him to dishonor his mother *at all,* especially in public, would be breaking one of the Ten Commandments: "Honor your father *and your mother* that your days may be long in the land which the LORD your God gives you" (Exodus 20:12). Hence, while it would certainly be unusual for a Jewish man to address his mother as "Woman," Jesus does so in a way that is respectful and in accordance with the Torah.

Why then does Jesus address Mary as "Woman"? Although the Gospel does not explain this mysterious form of address, many modern biblical scholars suggest that in a Jewish context the word "Woman" may be an allusion to the figure of Eve in the book of Genesis. Before the Fall, Eve is referred to as "Woman" some eleven times (Gen 2:22, 23; 3:1, 2, 4, 6, 12, 13 (2x), 15, 16). As New Testament scholar Raymond Brown puts it, "The term would be intelligible" if Mary is being likened to "Eve, the 'woman' of Gen iii 15."

With this background in mind, we can now turn to Jesus' words: "What is that to you and to me, Woman?" (John 2:4). Some English translations of the Bible make Jesus' response sound much harsher than it is in the original language. Literally translated, his words are "What to me and to you?" (Greek *ti emoi kai soi*.) Because it is so terse, the meaning of this biblical expression has to be determined by its context and tone. In some cases it seems to mean "What have I done to you that you should do this to me?" (see Judges 11:12; Mark 1:24; 5:7). In other cases it seems to mean, "What concern is this matter to us?" (2 Kings 3:13; 2 Chronicles 35:21; 2 Samuel 16:10). For our purposes here, what matters most is that although the expression is not necessarily disrespectful, whenever it is used it indicates some kind of *refusal* or resistance to the intentions of one person by the other. Therefore, when we take seriously the fact that in our case Jesus' words are both an indication of some kind of refusal and the words of a Jewish rabbi to his Jewish mother, it seems that the best interpretation is that Jesus is firmly but respectfully declining some aspect of Mary's words.

If Jesus is refusing Mary something, the question arises: What is he refusing? And why? At first glance, he might seem to be unwilling to solve the problem of the lack of wine. But that can't be the answer, since he goes on to do just that when he instructs the servants to fill the jars with water, and then changes the water into wine. Moreover, if all he was refusing to do was perform a miracle, we would still be left scratching our heads about the reason he gives: "My hour has not yet come." So what exactly is he declining?

Mary's Words and the Wine of YHWH's Banquet

To answer this question, we also have to put Mary's words, "They have no wine" (John 2:3), in their original Jewish context.

On the one hand, Mary seems to be making a simple request that Jesus solve the problem of a lack of wine at a wedding. In an ancient Jewish context, it was customary for a wedding celebration to last not one day, not two days, but an *entire week*—"seven days" of feasting and joyful celebration (Genesis 29:22–27; Judges 14:17). Then, as now, wine was the celebratory drink of choice (Psalm 104:15). In our day and age, any bride or mother of the bride who has been involved in planning a wedding reception knows that providing enough food and drink to keep people satisfied for just a few hours is a major undertaking. Imagine what was involved in hosting a celebration that lasted an entire week! Hence, when the Gospel tells us that "the wine failed" at the wedding in Cana (John 2:3), it's the kind of problem that an attentive mother would have noticed. As a result, by saying, "They have no wine" (John 2:3), Mary brings the situation to Jesus' attention, as a kind of implicit request for him to fix the problem. As New Testament scholar Craig Keener says, "Simply stating the need, as she does, is an adequately explicit request."

On the other hand, as we've already pointed out, if this is *all* Mary is asking for, then Jesus' response to her doesn't quite make sense. For he goes on to do exactly what she "asks" of him by fixing the problem of the wine. Why? Once again, the answer may lie in the Old Testament. From an ancient Jewish perspective, Mary's words are not just an observation about this particular Jewish wedding; they also appear to be *an allusion to Jewish Scripture*. Like John the Baptist's allusion to Jeremiah, Mary's statement—"they have no wine"—is strikingly similar to a prophecy of Isaiah, which describes the people of Israel's desire for the wine of salvation:

> The wine mourns, the vine languishes, all the merry-hearted sigh. . . . *No more do they drink wine with singing. . . . There is an outcry in the streets for lack of wine;* all joy has reached its eventide; the gladness of the earth is banished. (Isaiah 24:7, 9, 11)

Now, if Mary is alluding to the book of Isaiah, then the implications are enormous, for the prophecy does not end with Israel running out of wine. In response to the people's lack of wine, Isaiah prophesies that the Lord himself will respond by giving them, at some point in the future, a very special feast of wine:

> *On this mountain the LORD of hosts will make for all people a feast of fat things, a feast of fine wine, of fat things full of marrow, of fine wine well refined.* And he will destroy on this mountain the covering that is cast over all peoples, the covering that is cast over all nations. He will swallow up death for ever, and the Lord GOD will wipe away tears from all faces, and the reproach of his people he will take away from all the earth. (Isaiah 25:6–8)

This prophecy is the most famous description in the Old Testament of what would later come to be known as "the messianic banquet." However, notice that in the book of Isaiah, the Messiah is not actually mentioned: it is the Lord (Hebrew *YHWH*) who gives the wine of the banquet. Notice also three striking features of this particular feast. First, it will be a sacrificial banquet of wine. That is what Isaiah means when he talks about "fat things" and "fine wines." In the Jewish Temple, both the fat of the sacrifices and fine wine were offered to God as bloody and unbloody sacrifices (see Leviticus 3:16; 23:13). Second, it will be a universal banquet, for both Israel and the Gentiles. That is what Isaiah means when he says that "all peoples" will be invited. Third and finally, it will be a banquet that will undo the effects of the Fall of Adam and Eve, for by means of God's banquet, death itself will be "swallowed up," and the sins of all the redeemed will be taken away.

Significantly, in later Jewish tradition, it came to be believed that this feast of God would be a kind of return to Eden, in which the righteous would drink *miraculous* wine that had its origins at the very dawn of time. As one ancient rabbinic tradition puts it:

> In the hereafter the Holy One, blessed be He, will prepare a feast for the righteous in the Garden of Eden.... The Holy One, blessed be He, will therefore in the hereafter give them to drink of *the wine that is preserved in grapes since the six days of Creation.* (*Numbers Rabbah* 13:2)

When we look at Mary's words—"They have no wine"—in the light of the prophecies of Isaiah about Israel's lack of wine and the Jewish hope for the wine of the banquet of YHWH, a good case can be made that she is alluding to this ancient Jewish hope for the miraculous wine of the banquet of YHWH. To be sure, she is implicitly asking Jesus to perform a miracle. But it's not just any miracle that she's asking for. She's asking that Jesus provide the sacrificial and supernatural wine of salvation spoken of by the prophet Isaiah and long awaited by the Jewish people.

If this interpretation of Mary's words is correct, then all of a sudden Jesus' otherwise baffling response, "My hour has not yet come" (John 2:4)—in which he appears to refuse her invitation—suddenly begins to make sense, in at least three ways.

Jesus and the Wine of the Messiah

First, by performing a miracle in which he provides miraculous wine, Jesus is beginning to reveal his identity as the long-awaited Jewish Messiah.

In order to see this clearly, it is important to emphasize not just the miraculous nature of the transformation of water into wine, but the *amount* of wine produced. According to the Gospel of John, Jesus goes far beyond just solving the problem of the lack of some wine for the wedding guests at Cana. In carrying out the miracle, he specifically instructs the servants to fill to the top the "six stone jars" used for the Jewish rites of purification, "each holding *twenty or thirty* gallons" (John 2:6). If we do the math, it totals up to somewhere between 120 and 180 gallons of wine! Even in our own day, when wine is cheap and accessible, that's a lot of wine.

From an ancient Jewish perspective, the sheer amount of wine provided by Jesus would call to mind the fact that in Jewish Scripture, one of the marks of the future age of salvation is that it would be characterized by superabundant wine:

> In that day I will raise up the booth of David that is fallen. . . .
> *The mountains shall drip sweet wine, and all the hills shall flow with
> it.* (Amos 9:11, 13)

And in that day the mountains shall drip sweet wine . . . and all the stream beds of Judah shall flow with water; and a fountain shall come forth from the house of the LORD. (Joel 3:18)

Indeed, according to ancient Jewish tradition outside the Bible, one of the ways you would know that the Messiah had finally arrived would be the miraculous abundance of wine:

And it will happen that . . . *the Messiah will begin to be revealed.* And on one vine will be a thousand branches, and one branch will produce a thousand clusters, and *one cluster will produce a thousand grapes, and one grape will produce a liter of wine.* (*2 Baruch* 29:1–2)

When Jesus' miracle is interpreted in the light of these ancient Jewish expectations of the superabundant wine of God's banquet, and ancient Jewish hopes for the future, we can see that in providing hundreds of gallons of wine for this small country wedding at Cana, Jesus is signaling to those who have the eyes to see that the ancient Jewish hope for the superabundant wine of the age of salvation is beginning to be fulfilled in himself.

Jesus Takes the Role of the Bridegroom

Second, by agreeing to provide the wine for the wedding, Jesus also begins to reveal that he is not just the Messiah; *he is also the Bridegroom.*

As a guest, Jesus was not responsible for providing the food and drink for the wedding party. This would have been the duty of the bridegroom of Cana and his family. This is another reason that Mary's implicit request is so odd. The logical person to whom she would naturally bring the problem would be the host, the bridegroom himself. But she doesn't. She goes to Jesus with the problem, and he solves it. However, because he does it secretly, he leads the steward of the feast to react to the miracle in a way that reveals its deeper meaning:

> When the steward of the feast tasted the water now become wine, and did not know where it came from (though the servants who had drawn the water knew), *the steward of the feast called the bridegroom* and said to him, "Every man serves the good wine first; and when men have drunk freely, then the poor wine; but you have kept the good wine until now." (John 2:9–10)

Although we don't know much about the details of the office of "steward of the feast," he seems to have been the ancient Jewish equivalent of a kind of headwaiter or modern-day wedding caterer. (In Greek, his name is *architriklinos,* which literally means "ruler of the table.") It would have been his responsibility to oversee the quality and purity of the food and drink at the wedding banquet, something very important to Jews because of the biblical laws of ritual purity (cf. Numbers 19:14–22; Sirach 32:1–2). When the steward at Cana tastes the water that has become wine, he does not call Jesus over to thank him, because he has no idea that the wine was provided by him. Instead, the steward calls "the bridegroom" (Greek *nymphios*)—whose name is never given—in order to praise *him* for having saved the "good wine" for last (John 2:9–11). The irony is that it was the *bridegroom's* responsibility to provide the wine, but it is *Jesus* who has actually done so.

In light of the steward's reaction, all of the pieces of the puzzle begin to fall into place. When Mary implicitly asks Jesus to provide wine for the wedding, she is not just asking him to solve a potentially embarrassing family problem. In a Jewish context, *she is also asking him to assume the role of the Jewish bridegroom.* As New Testament scholar Adeline Fehribach puts it: "When the mother of Jesus says to Jesus, 'They have no wine' (2:3), she places him in the role of the bridegroom, whose responsibility it is to provide the wine."

If Mary's implicit request is not just about the wine at Cana, but also about the wine of Jewish prophecy, then the implications of Jesus' action run even deeper. For, as we have seen already, in Jewish Scripture it is God himself who provides the wine of the banquet of salvation. And even more, as we saw in chapter 1, in Jewish Scripture it is God who is referred to as "the Bridegroom" of his entire people (e.g., Isaiah 62:4–6). When we combine the prophecies of the wine of YHWH with the prophecies of YHWH the Bridegroom, Jesus' actions at Cana lead us to conclude that by transforming the water into wine and assuming the role of the Jewish bridegroom, Jesus is also beginning to suggest that the prophecies of *the divine bridegroom* are being fulfilled in him. In the words of Adeline Fehribach:

> [An ancient reader] would have realized that Jesus' action of providing quality wine in abundance from the purification jars illustrated that he, in fact, accepted the role of the bridegroom, but that he was no ordinary bridegroom. . . . The sign Jesus performed illustrated that he was accepting the role of the messianic bridegroom, and that as such he was assuming the role of Yahweh, the bridegroom of Israel.

In other words, by means of the miracle at Cana, Jesus is beginning to reveal, in a very Jewish way, the mystery of his divine identity.

THE LAST SUPPER

Given everything we've seen so far, we can now ask the question: If Jesus is in fact the long-awaited Bridegroom of Jewish prophecy, and if he will indeed give the prophesied wine of salvation when his "hour" comes, then when exactly does this take place? When does Jesus give the wine of his wedding? Or, to put it another way, when is his wedding banquet?

The answer to these questions lies in the latter part of Jesus' response to Mary: "My hour has not yet come" (John 2:4). These words form a bridge between the sign of the messianic wedding performed by Jesus at Cana and the reality of the messianic wine that is given in the Upper Room and consummated on the cross. In order to see this connection clearly, we need to make three basic points about the Last Supper and the passion of Jesus.

The Last Supper and the "Hour" of Jesus' Passion

First, when Jesus responds to Mary by declaring that his "hour" has "not yet come" (John 2:4), this is not simply an enigmatic way of saying, "It's not yet time for me to reveal my identity." To the contrary, whenever Jesus speaks in the Gospels of his "hour" (Greek *hōra*), he uses the expression in a technical way to refer to *the time of his passion and death*. For example:

> "Now is my soul troubled. And what shall I say? 'Father, save me from *this hour?*' No, for this purpose I have come to *this hour.* Father, glorify thy name." (John 12:27–28; cf. John 17:1)

> [Jesus said to his disciples in Gethsemane:] "Are you still sleeping and taking your rest? It is enough; *the hour has come;* the Son of man is betrayed into the hands of sinners. Rise, let us be

going; see, my betrayer is at hand." (Mark 14:41–42; cf. Matthew 26:45)

In light of these passages, the meaning of Jesus' mysterious response to Mary finally becomes clear. In a brief and powerful way, Jesus is saying to Mary: "It is not yet time for me to provide the wine of the banquet of YHWH. I will provide that supernatural wine, but only at the hour of my passion and death." In other words, he declares that the hour has not yet come for him to give the wine of salvation, but out of respect for his mother's implicit request, he nevertheless performs a *sign* that points forward to the hour of his passion.

The reason that this language is so important for us to understand is that according to the Gospel of John, the "hour" of Jesus' passion—and, therefore, the time when he *will* provide the wine of salvation—*begins* at the Last Supper. Over and over again, in the Gospel of John, during his public ministry, Jesus speaks of his "hour" as something in the future, something yet to come. But when the Last Supper finally arrives, this is how John begins his account:

> Now before the feast of the Passover, *when Jesus knew that his hour had come to depart out of this world to the Father, having loved his own who were in the world, he loved them to the end.* And during supper, when the devil had already put it into the heart of Judas Iscariot, Simon's son, to betray him, Jesus, knowing that the Father had given all things into his hands, and that he had come from God and was going to God, rose from supper, laid aside his garments, and girded himself with a towel. . . . (John 13:1–4)

Notice three things about John's description of the Last Supper. First, John deliberately ties the arrival of Jesus' "hour" (Greek *hōra*) with the beginning of the Last Supper. Although sometimes we might be tempted to think that Jesus' passion only really begins with the scourging at the pillar or the carrying of the cross, from John's perspective, the "hour" begins with the supper from which Judas departs in order to betray him. Second, notice also that John describes the Last Supper as a banquet of *love*. Given everything we've seen so far about Jesus' identity as bridegroom, this is striking language: Jesus the Bridegroom celebrates a banquet of love—that is, a wedding banquet—as he goes to his passion and death. Third and finally, John tells us what kind of love Jesus is enacting now that his hour has come: it is "love to the end" (Greek *telos*) (John 13:1)—that is, total, self-sacrificial love—that Jesus is manifesting in his wedding hour.

We will come back to this language of "love to the end" in just a moment; for now we simply need note that when we compare the account of the wedding at Cana with this account of the Last Supper, Jesus' otherwise mysterious response to Mary—"My hour has not yet come" (John 2:4)—can be further explained. Although Jesus is *not* refusing to solve the problem of the lack of wine at Cana, he *is* informing his mother that it is not yet time for the wine of which she speaks: the wine of the messianic banquet, of the wedding of God and his people. Jesus will give the wine of salvation *at the Last Supper,* when the hour of his passion has arrived.

The Last Supper and the New Wedding Covenant

In support of this conclusion, it is critical to note that it is not only the Gospel of John that helps us to see the Last Supper as a wedding banquet. When the accounts of the words of institution given to us in the other Gospels (and in Paul) are read through ancient Jewish eyes, they reveal to us that at the Last Supper Jesus is not simply celebrating a new Passover. Through the wine of the Last Supper—which Jesus identifies as his blood—Jesus is also inaugurating the *new wedding covenant* spoken of by the prophets.

In order to see this, we need to look carefully at Jesus' words over the wine at the Last Supper in particular. Although the various accounts of his words differ in detail, they all have a common core focused on blood and covenant:

> "Drink of it, all of you; for this is my blood of *the [new] covenant, which is poured out for many for the forgiveness of sins."* (Matthew 26:27–28)

> "This is my blood of *the [new] covenant, which is poured out for many."* (Mark 14:24)

> "This cup which is poured out for you is *the new covenant* in my blood." (Luke 22:20)

> "This cup is *the new covenant* in my blood. Do this, as often as you drink it, in remembrance of me." (1 Corinthians 11:25)

Although the various versions of Jesus' words over the cup obviously differ in details, in all of them Jesus identifies the wine of the Last Supper with the "blood" of a new "covenant."

One reason this connection is important is that, as many scholars agree, any first-century Jew (such as the twelve disciples) hearing Jesus refer to the "blood" of the "covenant" would have immediately recognized in his words an allusion to the covenant between God and Israel that was made at Mount Sinai. In this regard, compare the words of Jesus at the Last Supper with words of Moses in the book of Exodus:

> And Moses took the blood and threw it upon the people, and said,
> "Behold the blood of the covenant which the LORD has made
> with you in accordance with all these words." (Exodus 24:8)

In other words, by identifying the wine of the covenant at the
Last Supper with *his* blood, Jesus is by definition speaking of the
new covenant that Jeremiah and the other prophets had foretold
God would one day make in place of the covenant that had been
sealed at Mount Sinai (see Jeremiah 31:31–33) but had since been
broken. Indeed, as one biblical scholar puts it, Jesus' actions at the
Last Supper are a kind of "new Sinai," in which he inaugurates a
new union between God and his people.

The reason all of this Jewish background matters for us is this:
If in his words over the bread and wine Jesus is alluding to the
blood of the covenant from Mount Sinai (Exodus 24:8) and the
new covenant of the prophets (Jeremiah 31:31–33), then from an
ancient Jewish perspective the covenant being established by Jesus
is a *marriage covenant* between the Bridegroom God of Israel and
the people of Israel. And if this is correct, then the Last Supper is
a *wedding banquet:* the wedding banquet of God and his people.

In support of this suggestion, here is one last observation. Unlike some of Jesus' other memorable meals (like the feeding of the
five thousand), the Last Supper is celebrated with the twelve disciples. Why? As Jesus himself says: because it is a *covenant* banquet:

> "You are those who have continued with me in my trials; as my
> Father covenanted a kingdom to me, so do I covenant to you
> that you may eat and drink at my table in my kingdom, and sit
> on thrones judging the twelve tribes of Israel." (Luke 22:28–30)

In other words, the reason Jesus celebrates the Last Supper with
the twelve disciples is that together they represent the bride of

God—the people of Israel. This is a prophetic sign whose symbolism would have been recognized by any Jew familiar with the prophecies of God's future wedding. Just as YHWH wed himself to the twelve tribes of Israel at Mount Sinai through the blood of the old covenant, so now Jesus unites himself to the twelve disciples through the blood of the new covenant, which is sealed in his blood. In the words of Claude Chavasse:

> In the Last Supper, [Jesus] was as much enacting a Marriage Feast as keeping the Passover. Essentially, the Passover itself was nuptial. The foundation of the Marriage between Yahweh and his People was the Covenant between them. . . . It is therefore no playing with words, but the sober truth, to say that Jesus, if not enacting *a* marriage at the Last Supper, was solemnizing *the* Marriage between himself and his Church in this, the New Covenant.

By means of this new covenant, Jesus reveals that *he himself* is the true Bridegroom, and the new Israel that will be established through his disciples is the bride of God. In this new wedding covenant it is no longer the blood of bulls and goats that will be poured out, but the blood of Jesus, who is the Bridegroom God of Israel come in the flesh.

Jesus Drinks the Wine of Consummation on the Cross

Third and finally, should there be any doubt about the connections between the "hour" of Jesus' Last Supper and the "hour" of his passion and death, or between the wine of Jesus' Last Supper and the wine of salvation, it is worth noting that both of these elements are fused into one during Jesus' final moments on the cross.

Not surprisingly, it is the Gospel of John that brings this to our attention. In his account of Jesus' death on the cross, John highlights the fact that Jesus' final action on the cross is to drink *wine*. In the unforgettable words of the Gospel:

> But standing by the cross of Jesus were *his mother,* and his mother's sister, Mary the wife of Clopas, and Mary Magdalene. When Jesus saw his mother, and the disciple whom he loved standing near, he said to his mother, "*Woman,* behold your son!" Then he said to the disciple, "Behold, your mother!" And from that *hour* the disciple took her to his own home. After this, Jesus, knowing that all was now finished, said (to fulfill the scripture), *"I thirst." A bowl full of common wine stood there; so they put a sponge full of the wine on hyssop and held it to his mouth. When Jesus had received the wine, he said, "It is finished";* and he bowed his head and gave up his spirit. (John 19:25–30)

In light of everything we've seen in this chapter, notice three things about this powerful and familiar scene. First, there are striking echoes here of Jesus' actions at Cana: just as Jesus addressed his mother at the wedding of Cana as "Woman" and declared that the "hour" had not yet come for him to give the wine of salvation; so now he addresses Mary as "Woman" and drinks the wine of Calvary before dying on the cross. Second, notice the echoes of the Last Supper. Just as Jesus' "hour" began at the Last Supper, when he "loved" his disciples "to the end" (Greek *telos*); so now he gives up his life after drinking the wine of the cross and declaring, "It is finished," or "It is consummated" (Greek *tetelestai*) (John 19:30). In this way, John reveals to us that not only is the Last Supper a wedding banquet, but the crucifixion is an act of love. It is the sacrifice of the Bridegroom Messiah, giving himself up for the sake of his bride. Third and finally, even the mention of the branch of "hyssop" establishes a connection between the Last Supper, which John ties to "the feast of Passover" (John 13:1), and the cross. For in the original Passover "a bunch of hyssop" was dipped in the blood of the lamb (Exodus 12:22); here a branch of hyssop is dipped in the wine of Calvary (John 19:29), and in this way, the hour of Jesus' wedding, the hour of the Last Supper, and the hour of his passion and death—his love to the end—are united into one.

Jesus the Bridegroom and the Wine of Salvation

To sum up what we've learned so far: when we read the Gospel accounts of the wedding at Cana, the Last Supper, and the crucifixion of Jesus through the lens of the ancient Jewish hope for the new covenant wedding of God and Israel, they reveal several things.

First, as John the Baptist declares at the very outset of Jesus' ministry, Jesus is not merely the long-awaited Messiah, the king of Israel. If one is truly to understand Jesus' identity one must recognize him as the Bridegroom of Jewish prophecy, for whom John prepares the people of Israel, the bride.

Second, when Mary, the mother of Jesus, invites him to provide the wine at the wedding at Cana, she too is implicitly requesting that Jesus take the role of Bridegroom Messiah and provide the miraculous wine of the wedding banquet of YHWH. In response to her words, Jesus declares that the "hour" for the wine of his wedding has not yet come; nevertheless, out of reverence for his mother, he provides a sign of the wine that is to come, and assumes the role of the Messiah by providing a super-abundance of miraculous wine.

Third and finally, when we come to the Last Supper and the passion of Jesus, everything changes. The hour has finally come for Jesus to give the supernatural wine of the banquet of YHWH. However, instead of changing water into wedding wine as he did at the wedding at Cana, Jesus now changes the wine into his blood—the blood of the new and everlasting marriage covenant. As Saint Cyril, bishop of Jerusalem in the fourth century A.D., declared:

> *Jesus once in Cana of Galilee turned the water into wine by a word of command at Cana in Galilee. Should we not believe him when he changes wine into his blood?* It was when he had been invited to an ordinary bodily marriage that he performed the wonderful miracle at Cana. Should we not be much more ready to acknowledge that to "the sons of the bridal chamber" he has granted the enjoyment of his body and blood? (Cyril of Jerusalem, *Mystagogical Catechesis* 4:2)

In other words, at the Last Supper Jesus gives his bride the greatest wedding gift he could possibly give: the gift of himself. This act of loving sacrifice that begins in the Upper Room and is consummated on the wood of the cross. *This wine,* the wine of the Last Supper, is the "fine wine" of the wedding of YHWH and Israel, because this is the wine of Jesus' own blood. *This wine* is the supernatural wine that will enable those who drink it to "swallow up death forever." And *this wine* is the wine through which YHWH will not only take away the sins of his people, but also unite them to himself forever, by making them sharers in the flesh and blood of Jesus.

Yet the wine of the Messiah is not the only key that unlocks the secret of Jesus the Bridegroom. In order to see more clearly who Jesus was and why he died, we also need to look more carefully through ancient Jewish eyes at the mystery of his bride, and at his gift of living water.

3

The Woman at the Well

U p to this point we've outlined the ancient Jewish idea of the Bridegroom God of Israel. We've also shown how Jesus was identified as the long-awaited bridegroom whose wedding banquet was the Last Supper. Now another question emerges: *If Jesus is the Bridegroom Messiah, then where is his bride in the Gospels?* Any wedding portrait would clearly be missing something if it featured only the groom. In the same way, our portrait of Jesus the Bridegroom would be incomplete if we did not also attempt to paint a clearer picture of his bride.

To be sure, we've already seen several clues to her identity. In chapter 1, we showed how Jewish Scripture clearly identifies the bride of God not as a single individual, but as the entire people of Israel, often symbolized by the city of Jerusalem. Taken together, all twelve tribes are the bride of YHWH, the "virgin Israel" (Jeremiah 31:4). In chapter 2, we saw that John the Baptist suggests that he is preparing the Jewish people as a "bride" for Jesus, the Messiah (John 3:28–29), and that Jesus himself celebrates the new wedding covenant with the twelve disciples, as representatives of the twelve tribes of Israel (Matthew 26:26–28; Mark 14:22–25; Luke 22:19–20, 29–30; 1 Corinthians 11:23–25). Taken together, all of this evidence leads us to the conclusion that the bride of Jesus, like the bride of YHWH in the Old Testament, is not a single individual, but rather *the entire people of God,* redeemed and gathered into one by the new covenant established in Jesus' blood. The bride of Jesus is the bride of God: the new Israel.

We could just stop there and leave it at that. But when we try to read the Gospels through ancient Jewish eyes, we begin to see that it isn't just the twelve male disciples who represent the new Israel, the bride of God. The *female disciples* of Jesus also on occasion stand out as *bridal figures*—symbols of the entire people of God who are to be united with him through the new covenant. Indeed, entire books have been written on the women in the Gospels and the way in which these individual women symbolize the bride of Jesus.

For our purposes, we will focus our attention in this chapter on just one of these women: the Samaritan woman at the well (John 4:1–42). As we will see, although she is clearly an individual person who comes to believe in Jesus as Messiah, when her encounter with him is read through the lens of Jewish Scripture and tradition, she takes on a role that is larger than life and becomes, in her words and actions, a symbol of the bride of Jesus. In particular, Jesus' words to her about "the living water" that he wishes to give her (John 4:7–15) can lead us into a deeper understanding of who the bride of Jesus is and how her sins are cleansed by his passion and death on the cross.

In order to see all this, we will have to look at this familiar account from the Gospels very carefully and try to see it through ancient Jewish eyes.

THE SAMARITAN WOMAN

Significantly, in the Gospel of John it is not long after John the Baptist delivers his riddle about Jesus being "the bridegroom" and himself the "friend of the bridegroom" (John 3:25–29) that Jesus encounters a woman who, from an ancient Jewish perspective, looks mysteriously like a bride (John 4:1–42). Although the Gospel account of Jesus' encounter with the Samaritan woman is somewhat long, it is worth examining closely, highlighting certain elements that will prove important for our study.

> [Jesus] left Judea and departed again to Galilee. He had to pass through Samaria. So he came to a city of Samaria, called Sychar, near the field that Jacob gave to his son Joseph. *Jacob's well was there, and so Jesus, wearied as he was with his journey, sat down beside the well.* It was about *the sixth hour. There came a woman of Samaria to draw water.* Jesus said to her, "Give me a drink." For his disciples had gone away into the city to buy food. The Samaritan woman said to him, "How is it that you, a Jew, ask a drink of me, a woman of Samaria?" For Jews have no dealings with Samaritans. Jesus answered her, "If you knew the gift of God, and who it is that is saying to you, 'Give me a drink,' you would have asked him, and he would have given you *living water.*" The woman said to him, "Sir, you have nothing to draw with, and the well is deep; where do you get that living water? *Are you greater than our father Jacob,* who gave us the well, and drank from it himself, and his sons, and his cattle?" Jesus said to her, "Everyone who drinks of this water will thirst again, but whoever drinks of the water that I shall give him will never thirst; the water that I shall give him will become in him a spring of water welling up to eternal life." The woman said to him, "Sir, give me this water, that I may not thirst, nor come here to draw."

Jesus said to her, "Go, call your husband, and come here."
The woman answered him, "I have no husband." Jesus said to
her, *"You are right in saying, 'I have no husband'; for you have had
five husbands, and he whom you now have is not your husband;* this
you said truly." The woman said to him, "Sir, I perceive that
you are a prophet. *Our fathers worshiped on this mountain; and
you say that in Jerusalem is the place where men ought to worship."*
Jesus said to her, "Woman, believe me, the hour is coming when
neither on this mountain nor in Jerusalem will you worship
the Father. You worship what you do not know; we worship
what we know, for salvation is from the Jews. But the hour is
coming, and now is, when the true worshipers will worship the
Father in spirit and truth, for such the Father seeks to worship
him. God is spirit, and those who worship him must worship in
spirit and truth." The woman said to him, "I know that Messiah
is coming (he who is called Christ); when he comes, he will
show us all things." Jesus said to her, "I who speak to you am
he." (John 4:3–26)

It will take most of this chapter for us to delve into this amazingly
rich account. For now, several questions need to be highlighted.
First, what is the significance of the fact that this encounter takes
place at "Jacob's well" (John 4:6)? Second, why does Jesus initiate
this exchange with a "Samaritan woman" (John 4:9)? The Samaritans were by and large despised and regarded as unclean by the
Jews; hence it would have been extremely unusual for a Jewish
man like Jesus to initiate a conversation with a Samaritan woman,
much less to ask her for a drink. Third, what is the meaning of
the conversation between Jesus and the Samaritan woman? In
particular, why do they spend so much time talking about "living water" (John 4:10–15)? And why does the conversation shift
from the discussion of this mysterious water to the Samaritan

woman's past, to the question of whether or not God should be worshipped in the temple on Mount Gerizim (as the Samaritans believed) or in the Temple in Jerusalem (as the Jews held)? What is going on here, and what does any of it have to do with Jesus the Bridegroom?

Once again, the answers to these questions can be found by going back to Jewish Scripture and tradition and looking at this episode in light of what these sources have to tell us about bridegrooms, brides, wells, and "living water."

Women, Wells, and Weddings in the Old Testament

As many scholars have recognized, from an ancient Jewish perspective the Samaritan woman looks suspiciously like *a potential bride*. Although it's easy for modern readers to miss this point entirely, the similarities would have been a lot clearer for ancient Jewish readers of John's account. They would have been privy to one key piece of cultural information: at the time of Jesus, if you were an eligible young Jewish man looking for an eligible young Jewish woman, you would not go to a bar or to a club. Instead, you would go where the ladies were to be found: the local well.

If you look carefully at Jewish Scripture, you will notice that on more than one occasion a future bridegroom (or his servant) first meets a future bride *at a well*. For example, in the book of Exodus, the prophet Moses meets his future bride at a well:

> But Moses fled from Pharaoh, and stayed in the land of Midian; and he *sat down by a well*. Now the priest of Midian had seven daughters; and they came and drew water. . . . Moses stood up and helped them, and watered their flock. . . . And Moses was content to dwell with [the priest of Midian], and he gave Moses his daughter Zipporah. (Exodus 2:15–17, 21)

Along the same lines, the unnamed servant of Abraham, whom Abraham sent to find a bride for his son Isaac, meets Isaac's future bride Rebekah at a well. In order to complete his quest, the servant prays to the Lord:

> "Let the maiden to whom I shall say, 'Pray let down your jar that I may drink,' and who shall say, 'Drink, and I will water your camels'—let her be the one. . . ." Before he had done speaking, behold, Rebekah . . . came out with her water jar upon her shoulder. The maiden was very fair to look upon, a virgin, whom no man had known. (Genesis 24:14, 15–16)

Finally, and most important of all, the patriarch Jacob—whose well Jesus is sitting beside (John 4:6)—meets Rachel, his future bride, at a well. In an ancient Jewish context this story would have functioned like a family tale of how your grandfather met your grandmother. With Jesus' encounter with the Samaritan woman in mind, reread the account of Jacob's encounter with his future bride:

> *Then Jacob went on his journey, and came to the land of the people of the east. As he looked, he saw a well in the field,* and lo, three flocks of sheep lying beside it; for out of that well the flocks were watered. The stone on the well's mouth was large, and when all the flocks were gathered there, the shepherds would roll the stone from the mouth of the well, and water the sheep, and put the stone back in its place upon the mouth of the well. Jacob said to them, "My brothers, where do you come from?" They said, "We are from Haran." He said to them, "Do you know Laban the son of Nahor?" They said, "We know him." He said to them, "Is it well with him?" They said, *"It is well; and see, Rachel his daughter is coming with the sheep!"* He said, "Behold, *it is still high day,* it

is not time for the animals to be gathered together; water the sheep, and go, pasture them." But they said, "We cannot until all the flocks are gathered together, and the stone is rolled from the mouth of the well; then we water the sheep." *While he was still speaking with them, Rachel came with her father's sheep; for she kept them.* (Genesis 29:1–9)

Notice several striking parallels between these Old Testament accounts and Jesus' encounter with the Samaritan woman. Just as Moses, Abraham's servant, and Jacob are male foreigners in a strange land, so too Jesus is a foreigner on Samaritan soil (John 4:4–6). And just as Abraham's servant asks Rebekah for a drink of water to find out if she is the bride (Genesis 24:14–21), so too Jesus asks the Samaritan woman: "Give me a drink" (John 4:7). And just as Jacob encounters Rachel at the well at "high day" or "midday" (Genesis 29:7), so too Jesus encounters the Samaritan woman at "the sixth hour," right around noon (John 4:6).

In light of these parallels—which would have been very well known by ancient Jews because these stories are from the Pentateuch—some biblical scholars point out that a basic pattern exists that would have been recognized by any ancient Jew:

Male Foreigner + Woman + Well = Betrothal

Indeed, although modern readers might miss the potentially nuptial implications of the scene, Jesus' disciples apparently do not. For when they return from the city, they are shocked at what they find:

Just then his disciples came. They marveled that he was talking with a woman, but none said, "What do you wish?" or "Why are you talking with her?" (John 4:27)

What are we to make of the disciples' reaction here? On numerous occasions Jesus talks with women, such as the Canaanite woman (Matthew 15:21–28), Martha and her sister, Mary (Luke 10:38–42), the woman with a hemorrhage (Mark 5:25–34), and the women who traveled with him and the disciples (Luke 8:1–3). In light of such evidence, it seems clear that the disciples are not surprised at the simple fact that Jesus is talking with a woman; they are surprised that *he is talking with a strange woman at a well*. Although the disciples are sometimes dense, they know Jewish Scripture well enough to figure out that this kind of encounter between a man and a woman usually leads to a wedding.

In short, Jesus' encounter with the Samaritan woman at the well is remarkably similar to the encounter between Jacob, the patriarch of Israel, and Rachel, the matriarch of Israel. As New Testament scholar Adeline Fehribach puts it, when compared with Jewish Scripture, the story of Jesus and the Samaritan woman "contains the initial elements of a betrothal type-scene."

The Samaritan Woman Is a Mixture of Israelite and Gentile

With that said, it's important to add that the Samaritan woman is no *ordinary* bride-to-be. On two counts her identity is at odds with the kind of woman one would expect a young Jewish man like Jesus to pursue if he were interested in an ordinary marriage.

For one thing, she is a *Samaritan,* and not a Jew. She herself highlights this point when she asks Jesus why he is asking her for a drink (John 4:9). In order to understand why she's surprised that Jesus initiates a conversation with her, we need to recall the historical origins of the Samaritan people. According to Jewish Scripture, in 722 B.C. the Assyrian Empire conquered the ten northern tribes of Israel and cast them out of the holy land, scattering them among the surrounding Gentile nations (see 2 Kings 17:21–23). In the place of the ten tribes of Israel, the Assyrians brought pagan Gentiles to dwell in the land:

> And the king of Assyria brought people from Babylon, Cuthah, Avva, Hamath, and Sepharvaim, and placed them in the cities of Samaria instead of the people of Israel; and they took possession of Samaria, and dwelt in its cities. And at the beginning of their dwelling there, they did not fear the LORD. (2 Kings 17:24–25)

As the Bible goes on to report, the Samaritans did eventually come to worship the God of Israel, but they continued to worship their own gods as well, in a kind of syncretistic mixture of Israelite and pagan religion (see 2 Kings 17:29–40). Later on, the Samaritans would eventually accept the books of Moses as Scripture, and they even built a temple on Mount Gerizim, where they offered sacrifices to the Lord, as the Samaritan woman herself mentions (John 4:20). In light of this situation, it's easy to understand why the Jewish people to the south might not have had the most positive feelings about the Samaritans. From their perspective, the Samaritans were a people whose blood was a mixture of Israelite and Gentile and whose rival religion was a mixture of Jewish and pagan beliefs. In this context, it is not surprising that it was not customary (or acceptable) for a young Jewish man to strike up a conversation with a Samaritan woman.

The Samaritan Woman Has a Sinful Past

Even more problematic for her potential as an ordinary bride, the Samaritan woman has already had multiple husbands. Jesus brings this to light when he invites her to go and call her husband:

Jesus said to her, "Go, call your husband, and come here." The woman answered him, "I have no husband." Jesus said to her, *"You are right in saying, 'I have no husband'; for you have had five husbands, and he whom you now have is not your husband;* this you said truly." (John 4:16–18)

The Gospel does not tell us why the Samaritan woman has been married so many times. Although it's possible that she was widowed more than once, five times would certainly be extraordinary (see, however, Tobit 3:8). Much more likely, she has been through multiple divorces. In the Torah, Moses gives a man permission to divorce his wife if he finds "some indecency in her" (Deuteronomy 24:1–4)—an obscure expression that later rabbis interpreted in different ways, ranging from finding her guilty of adultery to guilty of burning her husband's dinner (Mishnah, *Gittin* 9:10)!

Whatever the reasons, the main point is that the Samaritan woman has been divorced *five times.* Although in our own day and age serial divorce and remarriage is quite common, in the first century this pattern of behavior would have made her, to put it mildly, an extraordinarily unlikely prospect for another marriage. In the words of one first-century Jewish writing: "Do not add marriage to marriage, calamity to calamity" (*Pseudo-Phocylides* 205). Perhaps that is why she has been reduced to living with a man who is "not [her] husband" (John 4:18). In her current situation, she is in a socially undesirable and, from ancient Jewish perspective, gravely immoral state of public fornication (see Josephus, *Against Apion*, 2.199; Tosefta, *Sanhedrin* 13:8).

The Samaritan Woman Is a Symbol of Her People

What then are we to make of this strange encounter? On one hand, Jesus is deliberately initiating a conversation with an unmarried foreign woman in a way that would have seemed suggestive to any ancient Jew. On the other hand, Jesus cannot be interested in her for the usual reasons, given that he is, among other things, a celibate Jewish prophet and she is a five-time divorced Samaritan woman who is currently living with a man. What are we to make of Jesus' actions in this seemingly bizarre situation?

A number of biblical scholars have suggested that the Samaritan woman is also *a symbol of the people of Samaria, with whom Jesus wishes to enter into a relationship as Bridegroom and Messiah*. In order to see how this might have been the case in a first-century Jewish context, we need to make three basic points.

First, it is important to remember that Jesus is not the only Jewish prophet who ever entered into a strange relationship with a woman who was meant to represent her people as a whole. As I mentioned in chapter 1, long before Jesus, the prophet Hosea does just this when he marries the prostitute Gomer as a public sign of the spiritual harlotry and infidelity of the people of Israel toward God:

> When the LORD first spoke through Hosea, the LORD said to Hosea, "Go, take to yourself a wife of harlotry and have children of harlotry, for the land commits great harlotry by forsaking the LORD." So he went and took Gomer the daughter of Diblaim, and she conceived and bore him a son. (Hosea 1:2–3)

Along the same lines, the prophet Isaiah marries an unnamed prophetess and through her conceives a son that he names "The spoil speeds, the prey hastes" (Hebrew *Maher-shalal-hash-baz*) (Isaiah 8:1–4). Actions such as those of Hosea and Isaiah are referred to by modern scholars as "prophetic signs," and they are often deliberately designed to be shocking or bizarre in order to catch people's attention. Even more important, prophetic signs were supposed to set in motion whatever they symbolize—usually some act of God in salvation history. In the same way, Jesus' initiation of an encounter with the Samaritan woman at Jacob's well seems to be a prophetic sign symbolizing that the time has come when God will wed himself not only to the Jewish people, but to non-Jewish believers in YHWH as well.

Second, in support of this suggestion, in the same way that Hosea's harlot wife Gomer is a perfect match for the prophet to perform his sign, so too the Samaritan woman is a perfect fit. For with both the harlot Gomer and the Samaritan woman there is a striking parallel between the *personal* history of the individual woman and the *national* history of her people. As several New Testament scholars have pointed out, just as the Samaritan woman has had five husbands in the course of her life, so too the Samaritan people were known for having initially worshipped multiple male deities. In the biblical account of the history of the Samaritans, we read:

> So one of the priests whom they had carried away from Samaria came and dwelt in Bethel, and taught them [the Samaritans] how they should fear the LORD. But every nation still made gods of its own, and put them in the shrines of the high places which the Samaritans had made, every nation in the cities in which they dwelt; the men of Babylon made Succoth-benoth, the men of Cuth made Nergal, the men of Hamath made Ashima, and the Avvites made Nibhaz and Tartak; and the

Sephar'vites burned their children in the fire to Adrammelech and Anammelech, the gods of Sepharvaim. (2 Kings 17:28–31)

Amazingly, the male gods of the Samaritans were actually called "Baals"—the Canaanite word for "husbands" or "lords" (see Hosea 2:16). Although it is true that some scholars reject the association that has been made between the five nations of Samaria and the five husbands of the Samaritan woman because the passage from 2 Kings lists seven gods, not five, as Gerard Sloyan points out, two of the seven deities listed above seem to be female goddesses (or consorts). If that is correct, the number of male deities would be five: one for each of the five peoples of Samaria. In support of this suggestion, the first-century Jewish historian Josephus emphasizes the number five when he refers to the cults of the Samaritans (*Antiquities* 9.14.3).

Third and finally, if this tie-in with the Samaritan "Baals" is the reason the Gospel tells us so much about the Samaritan woman's past, then the fact that she is now living with a man who is not her husband also mysteriously corresponds to the religious history of the Samaritan people. According to Jewish Scripture, in addition to the five male gods that they worshipped, the Samaritans also worshipped a sixth deity: YHWH, the God of Israel:

They [the Samaritans] also feared the LORD [Hebrew *YHWH*], and appointed from among themselves all sorts of people as priests of the high places, who sacrificed for them in the shrines of the high places. So they feared the LORD but also served their own gods, after the manner of the nations from among whom they had been carried away. To this day they do according to the former manner . . . So these nations feared the LORD, and also served their graven images; their children

likewise, and their children's children—as their fathers did, so
they do to this day. (2 Kings 17:32–34, 41)

As Adeline Fehribach argues, in the light of this aspect of the history of the Samaritans, Jesus' words take on a whole new meaning: "Jesus' statement to the woman, 'the one you now have is
not your husband' (4:18), [is] a reference to YHWH. YHWH is
not a true husband of the Samaritan people because Samaritan
Yahwism has been tainted by the influence of the worship of the
false gods and because they are in schism with the Jewish people."
In other words, by means of Jesus' prophetic encounter with the
Samaritan woman, he is initiating the time when the people of
Samaria will be incorporated into the new Israel by being united
to the true Bridegroom: YHWH, the living God of Israel.

The Samaritan People Are Betrothed to the Bridegroom Messiah

Should there be any doubt about this, notice how the account
of Jesus' encounter with the Samaritan woman climaxes. He reveals his identity as Messiah to her—something he does during
his public ministry only in non-Jewish territory—and she goes
home to her people and brings them to believe in him:

> The woman said to him, "I know that Messiah is coming (he
> who is called Christ); when he comes, he will show us all
> things." Jesus said to her, "I who speak to you am he." . . . So the
> woman left her water jar, and went away into the city, and said
> to the people, "Come, see a man who told me all that I ever did.
> Can this be the Christ?" They went out of the city and were
> coming to him. . . . Many Samaritans from that city believed in

him because of the woman's testimony, "He told me all that I ever did." So when the Samaritans came to him, they asked him to stay with them; and he stayed there for two days. And many more believed because of his word. They said to the woman, "It is no longer because of your words that we believe, for we have heard for ourselves, and we know that this is indeed the Savior of the world." (John 4:25–26, 28–30, 39–42)

Remarkably, with these words we find yet another parallel with the betrothal stories from the Old Testament: just as Zipporah and her sisters went home to their pagan father, Jethro, and told him about Moses, so that Moses came to stay with them and be wed to Zipporah (Exodus 2:19–21), so too the woman at the well tells the Samaritans about Jesus the Messiah, and they come to faith in him as Messiah. And just as Rachel ran home to tell her father and family that Jacob was her father's kinsman, so that they might invite him to stay with them (Genesis 29:12), so too the Samaritan woman goes home to her kinsmen and tells them about Jesus the bridegroom, and they then invite him to stay with them. Through this encounter with Jesus the non-Jewish peoples of the world begin to be "betrothed"—so to speak—to the one who is both Bridegroom Messiah and Savior of the world.

THE GIFT OF LIVING WATER

But this is not the end of the story. Now that we have this biblical background in mind, we can focus our attention on the meaning of Jesus' otherwise puzzling words about giving the Samaritan woman "living water." If Jesus is the Bridegroom Messiah, and she is a bridal figure who represents the Samaritan people, then this might explain why he offers her a "gift":

> Jesus answered her, *"If you knew the gift of God, and who it is that is saying to you, 'Give me a drink,' you would have asked him, and he would have given you living water."* The woman said to him, "Sir, you have nothing to draw with, and the well is deep; where do you get that living water? Are you greater than our father Jacob, who gave us the well, and drank from it himself, and his sons, and his cattle?" Jesus said to her, "Everyone who drinks of this water will thirst again, but whoever drinks of the water that I shall give him will never thirst; the water that I shall give him will become in him a spring of water welling up to eternal life." The woman said to him, "Sir, give me this water, that I may not thirst, nor come here to draw." (John 4:10–15)

Even today, if a single man gives a single woman a gift, it's usually done for a very deliberate reason. (As any married couple knows, gifts take serious forethought on the man's part.) Indeed, even in our own day, if a man proposes marriage to a woman, he is only really taken seriously when he gives her the gift of a ring. Likewise, in biblical times, a bridegroom would make his intentions known by offering the woman a betrothal gift or "bridal gift" of some sort (Hebrew *mohar*). For example, when Abraham's servant realizes that Rebekah is 'the one' for Isaac, he immediately takes a gold ring and two bracelets and gives them to her as gifts (Genesis 24:22–27). Along similar lines, Jesus offers the Samaritan woman a gift—but not gold or silver. Instead, he offers "the gift of God," in the form of "living water" (John 4:10). What is the meaning of this strange expression?

This is one of the many occasions in the Gospels where the words of Jesus, when situated in their ancient Jewish context, can have more than one layer of meaning. Thus, in order to feel the full force of his words and try to hear them the way they might have been heard by a first-century Jew (or Samaritan, in this case), it is important to emphasize that the expression "living water" could have at least three different connotations in Jesus' day and age.

The Miraculous Water of Jacob's Well

First, on the most literal level, the expression "living water" (Hebrew *mayim hayyim;* Greek *hydōr zōn*) was simply an ancient Jewish way of referring to what we would call "running water." Such water was taken not from a standing reservoir or jar, but from a spring, from which a constantly replenished supply of water could be easily drawn and used for drinking and washing. At first this is exactly what the Samaritan woman takes Jesus to mean, when she says: "Sir, give me this water, that I may not thirst, nor come here to draw" (John 4:15). She wants flowing water that will never be used up, so she won't have to keep going back to the well.

At first glance this definition might not seem that significant, until we recall that in ancient Jewish tradition outside the Bible, Jacob's well was believed to have produced *miraculous living water.* In the ancient Aramaic Targums of the Jewish Scriptures, we find an expanded account of the story of Jacob's encounter with Rachel, in which he transforms the still water of the well into a spring that miraculously flows for twenty years:

> And when Jacob saw Rachel, the daughter of Laban, his mother's brother . . . *Jacob drew near and, with one of his arms, rolled the stone from the mouth of the well; and the well began to flow, and the waters came up before him,* and he watered the flock of Laban . . . and it continued to flow for twenty years. Then Jacob kissed Rachel, and raised his voice and wept. (*Targum Pseudo-Jonathan* on Genesis 29:10–11)

Notice the additional details here. In the biblical account, Jacob shows his strength by moving the stone that ordinarily took several shepherds to roll away (Genesis 29:3); in the Targum text Jacob does it with just one of his arms! (This wouldn't be the first time a man performed a feat of strength to impress a pretty woman.) In the biblical account, Jacob shows his spirit of service by watering Rachel's flock; in the Targum text, he transforms the well into a miraculous spring, which flows for twenty years. According to one other version of the story in the Targums, it was through "the merits" of Jacob that the well flowed (*Targum Pseudo-Jonathan* on Genesis 31:22).

The reason these ancient Jewish traditions about Jacob's miraculous well are important for us is that they provide a powerful explanation for the otherwise puzzling challenge posed to Jesus by the Samaritan woman: "Sir, you have nothing to draw with, and the well is deep; where do you get that *living water? Are you greater than our father Jacob,* who gave us the well, and drank from it himself, and his sons, and his cattle?" (John 4:11–12). Although we cannot be sure, the Samaritan woman seems to be familiar with the tradition that Jacob performed some amazing feat for Rachel involving "living water" at the well. As a result, she challenges Jesus to do the same for her. Little does she know that the water Jesus wishes to give her is even more miraculous than the running water that Jacob provided for Rachel.

The Living Water of the Temple

In addition to this first meaning, the expression "living water" is also used in Jewish Scripture to refer to the *ritual water* used in the Tabernacle of Moses and, later, in the Temple of Solomon, for cleansing and purification from sins.

For example, in the Torah, the Scripture teaches that when "living water" (Hebrew *mayim hayyim*) is combined with the ashes of a sacrificial sin offering, it has the power to cleanse a person from impurity, so that they can enter the sanctuary and worship God:

> For the unclean they shall take some ashes of the burnt sin offering, and *living water* shall be added in a vessel; then a clean person shall take *hyssop,* and *dip it in the water,* and sprinkle it upon the tent, and upon all the furnishings, and upon the persons who were there, and upon him who touched the bone, or the slain, or the dead, or the grave . . . *and he shall wash his clothes and bathe himself in water, and at evening he shall be clean.* (Numbers 19:17–20)

Notice that it is not just any kind of water that has the power to cleanse; the living water must be combined with the ashes of a *sacrifice* in order to transform it into holy water for use in the sanctuary. Notice also that a branch of "hyssop" is used to sprinkle the cleansing sacrificial water. Intriguingly, this is the same kind of branch used to sprinkle the sacrificial blood of the Passover lamb (Exodus 12:22). Finally, given Jesus and the Samaritan woman's discussion of right worship (John 4:20–24), it's important to emphasize that the reason a person is cleansed with the sacrificial living water is so that they can enter "the sanctuary of the LORD" in order to worship him (Numbers 19:20). Following this law, at the time of Jesus, large ritual baths known as *mikvaoth* were built outside the Temple in Jerusalem, so that Jewish pilgrims could be cleansed by water before entering into the Temple to offer sacrifice and worship God. (See John 11:55.)

The Living Water of the Jewish Bridal Bath

Third and finally, in an ancient Jewish context, the expression "living water" was also associated with *the custom of a Jewish bride undergoing a ritual bath before her wedding.*

This connection between living water and the ancient bridal bath can be found in both Jewish Scripture and ancient Jewish writings outside the Bible. For example, the Song of Solomon describes the bride on her wedding day as both a fountain and a well of living water:

> A garden locked is my sister, my bride,
> a garden locked, a fountain sealed . . .
> a garden fountain, a well of *living water,*
> and flowing streams from Lebanon.
>
> (Song of Songs 4:12, 15)

Even more striking is the ancient Jewish story of the wedding of Joseph and Aseneth, the daughter of Pharaoh. In this account, reflecting ancient Jewish custom, Aseneth the bride is instructed by an angel to wash in "living water" in preparation for her wedding:

> And Aseneth rose and stood on her feet. And the man [an angel] said to her, "Proceed unhindered into your second chamber and put off your black tunic of mourning, and the sackcloth put off your waist, and shake off those ashes from your head, and *wash your face and your hands with living water, and dress in a new linen robe as yet untouched and distinguished and gird your waist with the new twin girdle of your virginity.* And come back to me, and I will tell you what I have to say." And Aseneth hurried and went into her second chamber where the chests containing her ornaments were, and opened her coffer, and took a new linen robe, distinguished and as yet untouched, and undressed the black tunic of mourning and put off the sackcloth from her waist. . . . And she shook off the ashes from her head, and washed her hands and her face with *living water.* And she took an as yet untouched and distinguished linen veil and covered her head. (*Joseph and Aseneth* 14:12–17)

Amazingly, this ancient Jewish text uses the same Greek expression as the Gospel of John to describe the "living water" (Greek *hydati zōnti*) of the bride's wedding day. Clearly, in an ancient Jewish context, not only was "living water" used with reference to wells and the Temple; it was also used for the customary bridal bath. As one ancient rabbi says with reference to a Jewish bride: "Wash her, anoint her, have her outfitted, and dance before her, until she goes into her husbands' house" (*Aboth de Rabbi Nathan* 41).

When all of these connotations of living water are taken into account in our interpretation of Jesus' encounter with the Samaritan, suddenly his words take on a whole new meaning. When Jesus speaks of offering her a "gift," he is not talking about the ordinary betrothal gift, because he is no ordinary bridegroom. Instead of offering the Samaritan woman gifts of gold or jewels, he offers her "living water"—miraculous water, greater than that given by Jacob, water that will both cleanse her from her past sins and prepare her for the everlasting wedding feast of eternal life. On some level the Samaritan woman realizes this, since, as the Gospel of John tells us, after Jesus identifies himself as "the Messiah" of Samaritan expectation, she "left her water jar" and went into the city to proclaim him to others (John 4:28). Presumably, she is no longer looking for earthly water, but for something much more.

THE PIERCING OF JESUS' SIDE

Given this interpretation of Jesus' encounter with the Samaritan woman, we still have to answer one final question: When exactly does Jesus give the living water to the woman, since he (presumably) never sees her again? In order to answer this question and bring this chapter to a close, we need to try to build a bridge between Jesus' words to the Samaritan woman and his passion and death on the cross. We can do this by making three key observations.

The Living Water from the Heart of Jesus

First, on another occasion during his public ministry, Jesus identifies *himself* as the source of living water.

In order to see this, we need to connect Jesus' statement to the Samaritan woman with the one other instance in the Gospels in which Jesus speaks about "living water." According to the Gospel of John, on the last day of the Jewish Feast of Tabernacles—the fall harvest festival (Leviticus 23:34–36)—Jesus stands up in the Temple in Jerusalem and proclaims:

> "*If any one thirst, let him come to me and drink.* He who believes in me, as the scripture has said, '*Out of his heart shall flow rivers of living water.*'" (John 7:37–38)

There is much that could be said about this remarkable passage. Since the time of Origen in the third century A.D., commentators have debated whether or not the living water described by Jesus flows from the heart of the one who believes in him, or from the heart of Jesus himself. The Greek text, taken by itself, can be translated either way. However, as we will see in a moment, when the passage is placed in the larger context of John's Gospel, it seems clear—as many scholars argue—that the primary meaning of the passage refers to the waters flowing from the heart of Jesus. This conclusion sheds light on Jesus' words to the Samaritan woman: the reason she should ask *him* for "living water" is that he himself will be the source of the living water (John 4:10).

The Living Water from the Side of the Temple

Second, and equally important, when Jesus speaks about rivers of "living water" flowing from his heart, he says that this will take place "as the scripture has said" (John 7:38). While there is no single passage in the Jewish Bible that speaks of water flowing from someone's heart, Jewish Scripture does speak of a river of living water that will flow out of the side of the Temple in the future age of salvation.

For example, the book of Ezekiel climaxes with an amazing vision of "water" flowing out of the side of the future "temple" (see Ezekiel 47:1–12). This is clearly no ordinary water, since it grows from a stream into a mighty river, and wherever it goes "everything will live" (Ezekiel 47:9). Perhaps even more striking is the vision of the prophet Zechariah, who connects the flowing of this river from Jerusalem with the death of the Messiah:

> And I will pour out on the house of David and the inhabitants of Jerusalem a spirit of compassion and supplication, *so that, when they look on him whom they have pierced, they shall mourn for him, as one mourns for an only child.* . . . *On that day the mourning in Jerusalem* will be as great as the mourning for Hadadrimmon in the plain of Megiddo. The land shall mourn, each family by itself; the family of the house of David by itself, and their wives by themselves; the family of the house of Nathan by itself, and their wives by themselves; the family of the house of Levi by itself, and their wives by themselves; . . . all the families that are left, each by itself, and their wives by themselves. *On that day there shall be a fountain opened for the house of David and the inhabitants of Jerusalem to cleanse them from sin and uncleanness.* . . . *On that day living waters shall flow out from Jerusalem,* half of them to the eastern sea and half of them to the western sea; it shall continue in summer as in winter. (Zechariah 12:10–13:1, 14:8)

It is virtually impossible to overestimate the importance of these prophecies of the river of living water from Jerusalem for the interpretation of Jesus' words to the Samaritan woman and our understanding of his passion and death. Recall that much of Jesus' discussion with the Samaritan about the living water explicitly revolves around worship in the Temple. From her point of view, true worship takes place in the temple at Mount Gerizim; from the Jewish point of view, true worship takes place in the Temple in Jerusalem. But by speaking of the living water, Jesus points *forward* to the fulfillment of the biblical prophecies, in which there will be a new temple, new worship, and a river of living water flowing out of that temple to cleanse the people of God from their sins.

The Water from the Side of the Crucified Jesus

Third and finally, when we put these two things together—Jesus as the source of living water and the biblical prophecies of a river of living water flowing from the side of the Temple—suddenly, the deeper meaning of John's description of Jesus' crucifixion and death becomes clear. With Jesus' words to the Samaritan woman in mind, reread John's account of the aftermath of Jesus' death on the Cross:

> After this Jesus, knowing that all was now finished, said (to fulfill the scripture), *"I thirst."* A bowl full of common wine stood there; so they put a sponge full of the wine on hyssop and held it to his mouth. When Jesus had received the wine, he said, "It is finished"; *and he bowed his head and gave up his spirit.* Since it was the day of Preparation, in order to prevent the bodies from remaining on the cross on the sabbath (for that sabbath was a high day), the Jews asked Pilate that their legs might be broken, and

that they might be taken away. . . . But when they came to Jesus and saw that he was already dead, they did not break his legs. *But one of the soldiers pierced his side with a spear, and at once there came out blood and water.* He who saw it has borne witness—his testimony is true, and he knows that he tells the truth—that you also may believe. *For these things took place that the scripture might be fulfilled,* "Not a bone of him shall be broken." And again another scripture says, *"They shall look on him whom they have pierced."* (John 19:28–37)

Just as in the last chapter we saw connections between Calvary and Cana, so now, once the ancient Jewish background is in place, the links between Jesus' encounter with the Samaritan woman and his crucifixion become clear. Just as Jesus thirsted beside Jacob's well for water, so now he commences his final moments on the cross with the words "I thirst." And just as Jesus promised to give the Samaritan woman, and all who believe, "the living water" spoken of in Jewish Scripture, so now through his death on the cross, Jesus gives up both his "spirit" and the "water" that flows from his pierced side. In this way Jesus the Bridegroom washes away the sins of the people of God—the bride of God—with the living water flowing from the side of the true temple. Indeed, the Gospel of John calls our attention to Zechariah's prophecy of "him whom they have pierced," which, as we saw just a moment ago, is nothing less than a prophecy of the river of "living water" that would flow out of Jerusalem to cleanse the people of God from sin (Zechariah 12:10–13:1).

The Samaritan Woman and the Water of Baptism

In sum, when we look through ancient Jewish eyes at Jesus' encounter with the Samaritan woman, his words in the Temple about the living water, and the account of his death on the cross, it becomes clear that the bridegroom figure at the well is both the long-awaited Messiah and the divine Bridegroom, who comes into this world to enter into a covenant with both the people of Israel *and* the non-Jewish peoples of the world. The bridal figure, the Samaritan woman, represents the people of God. As Saint Augustine, the fourth-century African bishop of Hippo, wrote many centuries ago:

> It is pertinent to the image of the reality that this [Samaritan] woman, *who bore the type of the church,* comes from strangers, for the church was to come from the Gentiles, an alien from the race of the Jews. *In that woman, then, let us hear ourselves, and in her acknowledge ourselves and in her give thanks to God for ourselves.* (Augustine, *Tractates on the Gospel of John,* 15:10)

In other words, Jesus' encounter with the Samaritan woman demonstrates that the new covenant will be made with saint and sinner alike, Jew and Gentile. In the Samaritan woman, the Bridegroom God of Israel reveals his intentions toward all the nations of the world, and toward every sinner, no matter who they are, where they come from, or what they've done. They, like she, need only ask for the gift of living water, and it will be given.

Moreover, if the Samaritan woman is both a bridal figure and a symbol of the new people of God, then we can finally answer the question of when and how Jesus gives to her the living water. Strikingly, in the Gospel of John itself, Jesus' words to the Samaritan woman are preceded by a number of texts that are focused on *baptism*: the "Spirit" descends on Jesus during his baptism "with water" by John (John 3:32-33); Jesus declares to Nicodemus that one must be born "of water and spirit" to see the kingdom of God (John 3:5); and the immediate context of the encounter with the Samaritan woman is the *only* reference in the Gospels to Jesus being with his disciples while they are "baptizing" (John 3:25-26; 4:1-2). In the words of Saint Methodius, the ancient Christian bishop of Olympus:

> In the faith of the holy woman is pictured all the features of the church in true colors that do not grow old; *for the way in which the woman denied a husband when she had many, is just the way the church denied many gods, like husbands, and left them and became betrothed to one Master in coming forth from the water.* She had five husbands and the sixth she did not have; and leaving the five husbands of impiety, she now takes Thee, as the sixth, as she comes from the water, exceeding great joy and redemption.... *The espoused church of the nations, then, left these things, and she hurries here to the well of the baptismal font and denies the things of the past, just as the woman of Samaria did;* for she did not conceal what had formerly been true from Him who knows all in advance, but she said, "... Even if I formerly had husbands, I do not now wish to have these husbands which I did have; for now I possess Thee who hast now taken me in Thy net; and I am by faith rescued from the filth of my sins that I may receive exceeding great joy and redemption." (Romanus Methodus, *Kontakion on the Woman of Samaria* 9:11–12, 14)

In other words, the way the living water that flowed from the side of Jesus crucified reaches his bride is through the cleansing waters of baptism. By means of this water, all believers, prefigured by the Samaritan woman, become part of the bride of Jesus, the people of God, gathered from both Israel and the Gentile nations. That is the true nuptial bath by which the Bridegroom Messiah will cleanse his bride.

4

The Crucifixion

With all of this in mind, another question arises: *If Jesus is the Bridegroom Messiah and the sinful human race is his bride-to-be, then when exactly is his wedding day? And how is he married to his bride?* Given everything we've seen so far about the Last Supper being his wedding banquet and the water from his side the nuptial bath, the reader has probably already guessed the answer: Jesus' wedding day is the day of his death, the day of his crucifixion.

Yet I would venture to guess that this is not how most people think about the crucifixion of Jesus. For some, like the Roman soldiers who carried it out, the crucifixion of Jesus of Nazareth was primarily (if not exclusively) an execution. As we will see in a moment, Jesus was neither the first nor the last of many first-century Jews who met their end hanging from what the Romans called "the tree of shame." For those who think Jesus was primarily a great prophet or teacher, the crucifixion is a martyrdom. From this point of view, Jesus was an innocent man who gave up his life for justice and truth, dying for what he believed in. For most Christians, who see with the eyes of faith that Jesus is the Messiah and the Son of God, the crucifixion was a sacrifice for the sins of humanity. In Jesus' own words: "the Son of man came not to be served but to serve, and to give his life as a ransom for many" (Matthew 20:28; cf. Mark 10:45). But none of these notions gets us quite all the way to the idea that the crucifixion was also a *marriage*. In what sense can it be described in this way? What possible resemblance could there be between the brutal and bloody methods of Roman crucifixion and the beauty and joy of a wedding?

In this chapter we will try to answer this question by viewing the death of Jesus on the cross in light of ancient Jewish wedding traditions. In order to do so, we will have to take three basic steps. First, we will briefly examine the one saying of Jesus in which he explicitly identifies himself as "the bridegroom" and implies that his wedding day will be the day of his death. This will give us the opportunity to familiarize ourselves with certain ancient Jewish wedding customs. Second, we will take some time to learn about the brutal historical reality of an ancient Roman crucifixion, in order to flesh out exactly what happened to Jesus on Good Friday. Third and finally, we will then combine what we know about ancient Jewish weddings with what we've learned about Roman crucifixion in order to try to see the crucifixion of Jesus as the consummation of his spousal love for his bride and the realization of the supernatural marriage between God and mankind.

JESUS' WEDDING DAY

As I mentioned in the introduction, over the centuries many a man has jokingly referred to his wedding day as his funeral. But Jesus of Nazareth is the only man who ever described his *funeral* as his wedding day. He does so in what is arguably one of his most mysterious sayings—the parable about the "Sons of the Bridechamber."

While I suspect that many readers are familiar with the parable of the Sower, or the Prodigal Son, or the Good Samaritan—for our study of Jesus the Bridegroom, the parable of the Sons of the Bridechamber stands out as one of the most important passages in the Gospels. It is the only passage in which Jesus explicitly refers to *himself* as "the bridegroom" (Mark 2:19). Up to this point, we've seen John the Baptist identify Jesus as the Bridegroom Messiah. And we've seen Mary invite Jesus to act like the bridegroom. But in order to understand what Jesus might have meant by accepting this role, we need to look carefully at what he himself had to say about this aspect of his identity.

The Question About Fasting and Jesus' Mysterious Response

According to the Gospels of Matthew, Mark, and Luke, Jesus delivers the parable of the Sons of the Bridechamber in response to a question put to him about his disciples (Matthew 9:14–17; Mark 2:18–22; Luke 5:33–38). Although the teaching is recorded in all three Synoptic Gospels, for the sake of space, I will focus here on Mark's account:

> Now John's disciples and the Pharisees were fasting; and people came and said to him, "Why do John's disciples and the disciples of the Pharisees fast, but your disciples do not fast?" (Mark 2:18)

In order to put this question in its Jewish context, it's important to remember that fasting—deliberately going without food and drink for an extended period of time—was an important part of Jewish practice and belief at the time of Jesus. As the Gospels make clear, John the Baptist followed a pretty spare diet of wild bugs and honey, and presumably his disciples also fasted as a matter of routine (Matthew 3:4; Mark 1:6). As for the Pharisees, the most influential Jewish religious group of Jesus' day, we know from elsewhere in the Gospels that it was customary for them to fast at least "twice a week" (Luke 18:12). Apparently, in stark contrast to the public fasts of the Pharisees, Jesus' disciples aren't known for fasting, so he gets questioned on this matter.

Now, Jesus could have just said, "My disciples don't have to fast, because I say so," and that might have been enough. Or he could have launched into one of his long discourses and used the opportunity to teach about the dangers of doing external acts of piety in order to be seen by others (compare Matthew 6:1–18). But he doesn't do any of these things. Instead, as good teachers love to do, he responds to their question with a question, a kind of riddle:

> And Jesus said to them, "*Can the sons of the bridechamber fast while the bridegroom is with them?* As long as they have the bridegroom with them, they cannot fast. The days will come, when the bridegroom is taken away from them, and then they will fast in that day." (Mark 2:19–20)

What are we to make of this? Why doesn't Jesus just answer the question, instead of giving this cryptic riddle about a bridegroom, his friends, a bridechamber, and a wedding? Who is the bridegroom? What is a "son of the bridechamber" anyway? (This expression is often translated as "wedding guests"; see below for more discussion.) And although the sons of the bridechamber aren't fasting now, why is it that they will fast when the bridegroom is taken away? When will he be "taken away"?

As with the other bridegroom passages in the Gospels that we've looked at so far, in order to grasp the meaning of Jesus'

words, we first need to be familiar with Jewish Scripture as well
as the ancient Jewish traditions and customs which he is assuming
his audience will know. Nowhere is a familiarity with ancient
Jewish practice and belief more necessary than when one is trying
to make sense of the parables, in which Jesus often draws on the
realities of Jewish daily life—though often with an unexpected
twist. In order to grasp the meaning of any parable, you need to
be able to recognize both what is ordinary and what is unusual,
and then combine the two through a method of "comparison"
(Greek *parabolē*). In the parable of the Sons of the Bridechamber, Jesus is answering the question by drawing an analogy between himself and his disciples and the bridegroom and the male
members of an ancient Jewish wedding celebration. By means of
this analogy, Jesus is making at least three important points about
himself, his disciples, and his upcoming wedding.

Jesus Is the Bridegroom and the Wedding Is at Hand

First, Jesus clearly identifies *himself* as "the bridegroom" (Greek
ho nymphios) (Matthew 9:15; Mark 2:19; Luke 5:34). He does so
to suggest that the present time, while he and his disciples are
together, is like an ancient Jewish wedding feast: it's a time for
celebration, not for fasting.

   In order to feel the force of this analogy, we need to understand just how joyful an ancient Jewish wedding celebration was.
While it is true that weddings are happy occasions in all cultures, a good case can be made that ancient Jewish weddings were
particularly festive. Many modern-day wedding celebrations—as
elaborate as they may be—ordinarily happen over the course of a
single day or even just a single evening. By contrast, ancient Jewish wedding celebrations such as those described in the Bible ordinarily consisted of *seven days* of feasting with family and friends.

For example, according to the book of Genesis, after being tricked by his future father-in-law into marrying the wrong woman, the patriarch Jacob spends one "week" celebrating his marriage to Leah, and then one "week" celebrating his marriage to Rachel (Genesis 29:26–27). Likewise, it is on the "seventh day" of their wedding feast that Samson caves in and tells his Philistine bride the secret of the riddle with which he had stumped his guests (Judges 14:17–18). Finally, according to a Jewish text outside the Bible, at the wedding of Joseph and his Egyptian wife Aseneth, Pharaoh, the father of the bride, declares that anyone who does any work during the wedding week will be put to death:

> After this Pharaoh gave a marriage feast and a great dinner and a big banquet for seven days. And he called together all the chiefs of the land of Egypt and all the kings of the nations and proclaimed to the whole land of Egypt, saying, "Every man who does (any) work during the seven days of Joseph and Aseneth's wedding shall surely die." (*Joseph and Aseneth* 21:8)

If this text is any indication, ancient people took their wedding celebrations very seriously! A wedding was no time for fasting or for ordinary labor, but rather a time for feasting and celebrating. (Even in our day, Catholic weddings do not customarily take place during the season of Lent, because Lent is supposed to be a time for fasting and penance.)

In short, by means of his analogy, Jesus is identifying his public ministry with the Jewish wedding week, in which the bridegroom and his wedding party would celebrate together. As New Testament scholar Adela Yarbro Collins puts it: "The point of the comparison is that, just as one does not fast during a wedding, so Jesus and his disciples do not fast."

The Disciples Are "Sons of the Bridechamber"

Second, Jesus refers to his disciples as *the "sons of the bridechamber"* (Greek *huioi tou nymphōnos*), and he uses this identification as an explanation for why they do not fast (Matthew 9:15; Mark 2:19; Luke 5:34). To grasp the significance of this analogy, we need to understand both who the sons of the bridechamber were and how they functioned in an ancient Jewish wedding.

This is an excellent example of a saying of Jesus which can only be fully illuminated by Jewish tradition outside the Bible. For the expression "sons of the bridechamber" is nowhere to be found in Jewish Scripture. However, ancient rabbinic texts not only use the same expression as Jesus, they do so in almost the exact same context: a debate over whether members of a Jewish wedding party are required to perform certain ordinary religious obligations.

According to Jewish tradition, on a daily basis faithful Jews were supposed to tie small straps of leather known as phylacteries around their forehead and arms to pray the daily prayer that later came to be known as the *Amidah* (Hebrew for "Standing" prayer) (see Matthew 23:5). In addition, they were also to recite a famous passage from Scripture known in rabbinic literature as the *Shema'*: "Hear, O Israel: the LORD your God is one Lord; and you shall love the LORD your God with all your heart, and with all your soul, and with all your might" (Deuteronomy 6:4). With this in mind, compare the following rabbinic text with Jesus' words about the sons of the bridechamber not having to fast:

> Our Rabbis have taught: "The bridegroom, and the best man and all the sons of the bridechamber are free from the obligations of prayer and phylacteries, but are bound to read the *Shema'*." In the name of Rabbi Shila they said, "The bridegroom is free from, but the best man and the sons of the bride-

chamber are subject to the obligation." (Babylonian Talmud, *Sukkah* 25b–26a)

Notice how the rabbis lay out for us in very clear fashion the members of an ancient Jewish wedding party: (1) first, there is "the bridegroom" (Hebrew *hatan*); (2) second, there is the "best man" (Hebrew *shoshbin*); (3) and third, there are the "sons of the bridechamber" (Hebrew *beney huppah*). As the modern Jewish scholar Israel Slotki points out, although the last expression is sometimes translated as "wedding guests," the Hebrew phrase probably does not refer to everyone invited to the wedding. Instead, the sons of the bridechamber are "the friends of the bridegroom who prepared for him the bridal-chamber and attended on him at the wedding."

For our purposes, what matters most is that Jesus and the majority of the rabbis agree that the bridegroom and the sons of the bridechamber are *not* obligated to perform ordinary religious duties. Thus, in Jesus' parable, he is the bridegroom, the disciples are the sons of the bridechamber, and the time they are together during his public ministry is like the weeklong wedding celebration. Hence there is no reason for them to fast. In fact, we could go even further and suggest that for Jesus' disciples to fast while he is with them would amount to a denial of the fact that he *is* the bridegroom. In this way, the disciples' act of refraining from certain ordinary Jewish religious obligations becomes a kind of prophetic sign that Jesus is the long-awaited bridegroom spoken of by the prophets.

The Day of Jesus' Death Is His Wedding Day

Third and finally, Jesus also suggests that *the day of his death will be his wedding day.* Although the disciples cannot fast while the bridegroom is with them, Jesus concludes the parable by declaring that the time will come when his disciples will take up fasting: "The days will come, when the bridegroom is taken away from them, and *then they will fast* in that day" (Mark 2:20).

In order to unpack the meaning of this final part of the parable, it is important to understand that when Jesus speaks of the departure of the bridegroom, he is referring to one particular part of the seven-day wedding celebration: the night of consummation. As one rabbinic tradition puts it:

> A bridegroom is exempt from reciting the *Shema'* on the first night, or until the close of the [next] Sabbath if he has not consummated the marriage. (Mishnah, *Berakoth* 2:5)

On the night of consummation, the bridegroom would leave his friends and family and enter into what was known as the "bridal chamber" (Hebrew *huppah*) in order to be united to his bride, not to emerge again until morning. This aspect of ancient Jewish weddings is described in several places. For example, the book of Psalms says:

> In [the heavens God] has set a tent for the sun, which comes forth *like a bridegroom leaving his chamber* [Hebrew *huppah*], and like a strong man runs its course with joy. (Psalm 19:4–5)

In the book of Tobit (which is in Catholic and Orthodox Old Testaments but not in Protestant or Jewish Bibles), we find an even more explicit reference to the bridechamber. A young Israelite man named Tobias is to be married to a young Israelite woman named Sarah, whose first seven husbands have been killed on their wedding nights by an evil spirit (see Tobit 3:1–3; 6:9–17).

To save Tobias from certain death, the archangel Raphael appears to him and instructs him to perform a sacrifice in the bride-chamber on his wedding night in order to drive out the demon:

> But the angel said to [Tobias]:"... Now listen to me, brother, for she will become your wife; and do not worry about the demon, *for this very night she will be given to you in marriage. When you enter the bridal chamber* (Greek *ton nymphōna*), you shall take live ashes of incense and lay upon them some of the heart and liver of the fish so as to make a smoke. Then the demon will smell it and flee away, and will never again return. (Tobit 6:15–17)

Although this is certainly an unusual wedding night—most young bridegrooms do not begin their honeymoon by perform-ing what amounts to an exorcism!—it is an important window into ancient Jewish weddings. Although the wedding celebration lasted for a whole week, the climax of the wedding was the night of consummation, on which the bridegroom would consum-mate the marriage in the bridal chamber and not emerge until morning. It was only on that day—the wedding day—that the bridegroom would finally be separated from his groomsmen and be joined to his bride, leaving the sons of the bridechamber to "mourn" the loss of their friend.

With this background in mind, we can now see the deeper meaning of Jesus' parable. If Jesus is the bridegroom and his dis-ciples are the sons of the bridechamber, then the day on which he will be "taken away" from them can only mean one thing: *the day of his passion and death.* Although the disciples do not fast with him now, they will fast and mourn after he has been brutally put to death. In the words of New Testament scholar Craig Keener: "Jesus is the groom of God's people in the coming messianic banquet. . . . The 'taking' of the bridegroom, of course, is *a veiled reference to the impending crucifixion.*"

If this is correct, the implications of Jesus' parable are enormous. For although he is a bridegroom, on his wedding day, he will not be taken in joyful procession into an ordinary bridechamber. Instead he will be "taken away" by soldiers and guards—to the marriage chamber of the cross.

The Jewish Bridechamber and the Tabernacle

At this point you might still be wondering: Why would Jesus draw an analogy between the entry of the bridegroom into the bridechamber on the wedding night and the day of his death? Where would he get the idea for such a comparison?

One possible explanation may come from the symbolism of the bridechamber in Jewish tradition. Although the Bible tells us very little, according to the rabbis, the Jewish "bridechamber" (Hebrew *huppah*) was no ordinary structure; *it was designed to resemble the Tabernacle of Moses.* For example, according to one rabbi, the measurements of a bridechamber were supposed to match those of the holy of holies:

> If a man received it from his fellow to build him a *bridechamber*
> for his son . . . he must build it four cubits by six. . . . Rabbi
> Ishmael says: The height thereof should be half its length and
> half its breadth. The Sanctuary affords proof for this. Rabban
> Simeon ben Gamaliel says: Should all be according to the build-
> ing of the Sanctuary? (Mishnah, *Baba Bathra* 6:4; see 1 Kings
> 6:2–17)

Along similar lines, another ancient Jewish tradition describes the bridechamber as being decorated like the Tabernacle:

> As the bridal chamber is decorated with all kinds of colors, so
> was the Tabernacle decorated with all kinds of colors, "Blue,
> and purple, and scarlet, and fine linen" [Exodus 25:4], "That the
> spices thereof may flow" [Song 4:16]. (*Numbers Rabbah* 13:12)

In keeping with this ancient tradition, to this very day, in orthodox Jewish wedding services it is customary for young couples to
take their wedding vows beneath a portable "bridechamber" (Hebrew *huppah*) that is often designed to look like the Tabernacle.

If this symbolism of the bridechamber was present at the time
of Jesus, it provides a powerful explanation for why he chooses to
connect this image with his own passion and death. In short: *just
as God consummated the marriage to Israel in the Tabernacle of Moses
through the blood of the covenant, so too Jesus will consummate the marriage to his bride through the blood of the cross*. In the words of Saint
Augustine of Hippo:

> Like a bridegroom Christ went forth from his nuptial cham-
> ber ... He came even to the marriage-bed of the cross, and
> there, ascending it, he consummated a marriage. And when he
> sensed the creature sighing in her breath, he surrendered him-
> self to torment for his bride in a communication of love. (Au-
> gustine, *Sermo Suppositus,* 120:3)

What a stunning description of the crucifixion! Of course, this
nuptial interpretation of the Cross immediately raises the question: How can the death of one man bring about the marriage of
Creator and creature?

The answer: As we have already seen over and over again
in Jewish Scripture, it is the Lord, YHWH himself, who is *the*
bridegroom of his people. When seen through the eyes of Jewish
Scripture, Jesus' parable of the sons of the bridechamber may be

designed to reveal not only the nature of his death, but also the mystery of his divine identity. In the words of New Testament scholar Adela Yarbro Collins, Jesus' riddle "implies that the presence of Jesus is equivalent to the presence of God." Likewise, Sigurd Grindheim writes, "The clearest example of Jesus' use of a divine epithet [or title] is when he referred to himself as the bridegroom.... [T]his title is ... another expression of his self-understanding as God's equal. As the one who took God's place, he found a well-known description of God and applied it to himself." Finally, Joseph Ratzinger (Pope Benedict XVI) has this to say:

> Jesus identifies himself here as the "bridegroom" of God's promised marriage with his people and, by doing so, he mysteriously places his own existence, himself, within the mystery of God. In him, in an unexpected way, God and man become one, become a "marriage," though this marriage—as Jesus subsequently points out—passes through the Cross, through the "taking away" of the bridegroom.

Thus the parable of the Sons of the Bridechamber reveals not only that Jesus saw the day of his death as his wedding day; but also that, in a veiled way, his marriage is the divine wedding spoken of by the prophets. By means of this teaching, Jesus confirms what he symbolically enacted by taking the role of bridegroom at the wedding at Cana. He is not just the long-awaited Jewish Messiah; he is *the divine bridegroom in person,* come in the flesh to wed himself to his bride, the forgiven people of God.

WHAT WAS THE CRUCIFIXION LIKE?

Before we turn to the Gospel accounts of Jesus' death on the Cross and try to see it through the lens of an ancient Jewish wedding, it is important that we first take a few moments to familiarize ourselves with some of the gruesome details of Roman crucifixions in the time of Jesus, what they were really like, and how the crucifixion of Jesus would have been viewed by ancient Jews.

Many people these days are at least somewhat familiar with the ancient Roman form of execution known as crucifixion. For most, this familiarity primarily stems from reading the Gospels or from viewing popular depictions of the crucifixion of Jesus in art and film. On one hand, this kind of familiarity can be very helpful. On the other hand, because the crucifixion of Jesus is *so* familiar, it can also be easy to forget or to underestimate just how horrific this manner of execution really was, not to mention how shocking it would have been for Jesus (or the first Jewish Christians) to compare such a death to a wedding. Therefore, we need to highlight at least three aspects of Roman crucifixion in the first century that would have stood out in an ancient Jewish context.

The Cruelty of Crucifixion

First, the Roman practice of crucifixion was an extremely *cruel* form of execution. Both ancient Jews and Gentiles alike regarded it as nothing short of horrific. For example, the first-century Jewish historian Josephus refers to crucifixion as "the most wretched of deaths" (*War* 7.203). Along similar lines, the Roman jurist Paulus describes it as "the most severe punishment" possible (*Sententiae* 5.21.3).

One reason was that victims of crucifixion were ordinarily

prepared for the cross by scourging. For example, Josephus gives us this firsthand report:

> Many of the peaceful citizens were arrested and brought before Flaccus [the Roman consul], who had them *first scourged* and *then crucified*. (Josephus, *War* 2:306)

Unlike ancient Jewish flogging, which limited the number of whippings to thirty-nine or forty (see Deuteronomy 25:2; 2 Corinthians 11:24), Roman scourging had no such mercy. Moreover, Roman scourging preceding an execution (known in Latin as *flagellatio* or *verberatio*) was carried out with leather whips or thongs fitted with spikes or pieces of iron or bone specifically designed to tear the victim's flesh right off his body. Once again, Josephus tells us about an extreme case:

> *[He] had them scourged until their entrails were visible.* ... The men [were then] dismissed, all covered in blood, a spectacle that struck such terror into his menacing foes that they dropped their arms and fled. (Josephus, *War* 2:612)

As New Testament scholar Martin Hengel states in his classic study of crucifixion, "the flogging ... was a stereotyped part of the punishment [that] would make the blood flow in streams." Moreover, if the scourging itself did not kill the person condemned to death by crucifixion, he was often forced to carry the beams of the cross to the site of execution, and sometimes he was whipped along the way, causing even more wounds and drawing even more blood. By the time he was finally nailed to the cross, he would be a horror to behold.

After the preliminary scourging and whippings were over, the actual crucifixion involved some form of being hung on a wooden beam or "cross" (Latin *crux*)—whether by impaling, nailing, or tying the limbs with rope. For example, the ancient rabbis describe death by "hanging"—a common Hebrew way of referring to crucifixion—as follows:

> How did they hang a man? They put a beam into the ground and a piece of wood jutted from it. The two hands were brought together and it was hanged. . . . And they let it down at once: if it remained there overnight a negative command was thereby transgressed, for it is written, "His body shall not remain all night upon the tree, but you shall surely bury him the same day; for he that is hanged is a curse of God." (Mishnah, *Sanhedrin* 6:4, citing Deuteronomy 21:23)

It was in the practice of suspending the victim that the physical cruelty of crucifixion reached its height. In contrast to other forms of execution such as beheading, in which the person dies quickly, crucifixion was designed to make the victim suffer as long and as much as possible before finally dying. In the words of the Roman writer Seneca:

> Can anyone be found who would prefer wasting away in pain dying limb by limb, or letting out his life drop by drop, rather than expiring once for all? *Can any man be found willing to be fastened to the accursed tree, long sickly, already deformed, swelling with ugly weals on shoulders and chest, and drawing the breath of life amid long drawn-out agony?* He would have many excuses for dying before mounting the cross. (Seneca, *Epistle* 101 to Lucilius)

As Seneca's words show, in the end, the crucified man died of asphyxiation, suffocating under the weight of his own lacerated body. Because of the horrific and drawn-out nature of death by crucifixion, Roman authorities ordinarily erected crosses in places where the execution would be as public as possible. As the Roman author Quintilian writes: "Whenever we crucify the guilty, the most crowded roads are chosen, where the most people can see and be moved by this fear" (*Declamations* 274).

The Shame of Crucifixion

In addition to being extremely cruel, crucifixion was also widely regarded as the most *shameful* of deaths. Indeed, the famous ancient orator Cicero refers to the Roman cross as "the tree of shame" (Cicero, *Pro Rabiro* 16).

One reason that crucifixion was considered to be so shameful was that in the Roman Empire this method of punishment was used to execute members of the lower classes, such as slaves and foreigners (that is, non-Romans). Upper-class citizens, by contrast, were put to death by more "respectable" means, such as beheading. (For example, Saint Peter, a Jew from Galilee, was crucified upside-down in Rome, whereas Saint Paul, being a Roman citizen, met his death by decapitation.) As Cicero says: the cross is the "extreme and ultimate penalty *for a slave*" (*In Verrum* 2.5.169). In the words of another Roman writer, it was "the slaves' punishment" (Valerius Maximus 2.7.12). The very fact that a person was being crucified was a public declaration that he was nothing more than a slave of the empire, a nobody in the eyes of the world.

Moreover, the shame of crucifixion was increased by the deliberate mockery often involved. In the practice of crucifixion the executioners would often give full rein to their sadistic tendencies. As a result, some contemporary descriptions of the torture that accompanied crucifixion can make one shudder. Consider, for example, the eyewitness testimony of Seneca:

I see crosses there, not just of one kind but made in many different ways: *some have their victims with head down to the ground; some
impale their private parts; others stretch out their arms on the gibbet.*
(*Dialogue* 6.20.3)

In light of such evidence, New Testament scholar Craig Keener
concludes: "Although some features of crucifixions remained
common, executioners could perform them in a variety of man-
ners, limited only by the extent of their sadistic creativity."

Finally, and perhaps most shameful of all, according to Roman
custom, victims of the cross were normally crucified naked. As
one Roman author describes it:

A Roman citizen of no obscure station, having ordered one of
his slaves to be put to death, delivered him to his fellow-slaves
to be led away, and in order that his punishment might be wit-
nessed by all, directed them to drag him through the Forum
and every other conspicuous part of the city as they whipped
him. . . . *The men ordered to lead the slave to his punishment, having
stretched out both his arms and fastened them to a piece of wood which
extended across his breast and shoulders as far as his wrists, followed
him, tearing his naked body with whips.* (Dionysius of Halicarnassus, *Roman Antiquities* 7.69.2)

This last act of humiliation was meant to rob the crucified man
of any possible shred of dignity he might have left. Even modern Western sensibilities about modesty in clothing—which
are certainly not more stringent than those of ancient Jews or
Romans—restrict almost all contemporary depictions of crucifixions in film or in art from showing the Roman practice of
stripping the crucified.

The Mass Crucifixion of Jews

Third, because the crucifixion of Jesus is the only one that many people are familiar with, it's important to emphasize that he was not the first person to be executed in this manner. Most readers of the New Testament are familiar with the fact that Jesus was not crucified alone, but along with two "thieves" (Matthew 27:38–44; Mark 15:27–32; Luke 23:32–43). But many other Jews of his time suffered a similar fate, and mass crucifixions of Jews are documented from the period.

For example, in Egypt, the local leader Flaccus is said to have flogged and crucified some thirty-eight Jewish elders at one time as part of a "festival" in honor of the emperor (Philo, *Flaccus* 83–84). Moreover, the Jewish leader Alexander Jannaeus had eight hundred Pharisees crucified in the city of Jerusalem. To the horror of many, Alexander feasted and drank with his concubines while watching the victims being raised up on the crosses (Josephus, *Antiquities* 14.380; *War* 1.97). Right around the time of the birth of Jesus, the Greek governor Varus is reported as having crucified two thousand Jews at one time (Josephus, *Antiquities* 17:295).

Perhaps most stunning of all, according to Josephus, who was an eyewitness, the Roman general Titus is reported to have crucified up to five hundred Jews per day during the siege of Jerusalem in A.D. 70. Josephus tells us that there were so many victims that the Romans ran out of trees for the bodies:

> When they [the Jewish fighters] were going to be taken (by the Romans), they were forced to defend themselves, and after they had fought they thought it too late to make any supplications for mercy: *so they were first whipped, and then tormented with all sorts of tortures, before they died and were then crucified before the wall*

of the city. Titus felt pity for them, but as their number—given as up to five hundred a day—was too great for him to risk either letting them go or putting them under guard, he allowed his soldiers to have their way, especially as he hoped that the gruesome sight of the countless crosses might have moved the besieged to surrender. "So the soldiers, out of the rage and hatred they bore the prisoners, nailed those they caught in different postures to the crosses, by way of jest, and *their number was so great that there was not enough room for the crosses and not enough crosses for the bodies.*" (Josephus, *War* 5:449–51)

Five hundred executions per day, for any length of time, is a horrific number. In the first century, crucifixion was a weapon of mass destruction.

In sum: In a first-century Jewish setting, the Roman practice of execution by crucifixion was widely considered to be one of the cruelest and most shameful ways a person could die. As such, it was hardly the kind of death that anyone would ever associate with the happiness of a wedding.

THE PASSION OF THE MESSIAH

With all of this in mind, we can now take our third and final step by asking: If crucifixion was so cruel and so shameful and so bloody, why would Jesus—or anyone else, for that matter—compare the event to a wedding day? And if so many hundreds, if not thousands, of Jews before and after Jesus suffered the same death on the wood of the accursed tree, then what makes Jesus' crucifixion different? Why is his crucifixion the only one in human history that anyone has ever described as a marriage, and what light does this shed on who he was, and why he died on the cross?

In this final section, we will try to answer these questions by focusing our attention on three key moments from his passion: (1) the crowning with thorns; (2) the casting of lots for Jesus' seamless garment; and (3) the piercing of Jesus' side. As I hope to show, each of these events when seen through ancient Jewish eyes, presents us with important parallels between the crucifixion of Jesus and the wedding day of a Jewish bridegroom. Indeed, I would suggest that the authors of the Gospels are inviting us to look beyond the *history* of Jesus' execution to the *mystery* of the Bridegroom Messiah's wedding day. Let's now look carefully at each of these moments in turn, from both vantage points.

The Crowning with Thorns

First, the Gospels make a point of emphasizing that not only was Jesus mocked by the Roman soldiers as would-be king of the Jews, but he was dressed as a king in order to be ridiculed:

> Then the soldiers of the governor took Jesus into the praetorium, and they gathered the whole battalion before him. And they stripped him and put a scarlet robe upon him, and plaiting a crown of thorns they put it on his head, and put a reed in his right hand. And kneeling before him they mocked him, saying, "Hail, King of the Jews!" (Matthew 27:27–29; cf. Mark 15:16–19; Luke 22:11)

> Then Pilate took Jesus and scourged him. And the soldiers plaited a crown of thorns, and put it on his head, and arrayed him in a purple robe; they came up to him, saying, "Hail, King of the Jews!" and struck him with their hands. Pilate went out again, and said to them, "Behold, I am bringing him out to you that you may know that I find no crime in him." So Jesus came

out, wearing the crown of thorns and the purple robe. Pilate said to them, "Here is the man!" (John 19:1–5)

On the level of simple history, the crowning with thorns and the clothing of Jesus in a royal-colored robe are meant as acts of personal and political mockery. As New Testament scholar Raymond Brown puts it: "the crown is part of royal mockery, like the robe and the scepter." By stripping Jesus of his own garments and arraying him as if he were a king, the soldiers are in essence saying to Jesus: "So you are a king! Well then, you should be dressed like one!" In other words, they are mocking his purported claim to be the Messiah—the long-awaited king of Israel.

The Jewish Bridegroom Wears a Crown on His Wedding Day

However, when we look at the crowning with thorns with the prophecies of the bridegroom in mind, something deeper is going on here. For as any first-century Jew would have known, kings were not the only ones who wore crowns in Jesus' day. According to Jewish Scripture and tradition, it was also customary for *the Jewish bridegroom* to wear a crown on his wedding day.

In modern times the way you identify the bridegroom is to look for the man wearing the fanciest tuxedo or the nicest suit at the wedding. In an ancient Jewish context the way you spotted the bridegroom was to look for the man with the crown. Consider the following texts:

> Go forth, O daughters of Zion, and behold King Solomon,
> *with the crown with which his mother crowned him*
> *on the day of his wedding,*
> on the day of the gladness of his heart.
>
> (Song of Solomon 3:11)

During the war of Vespasian [before the Temple destruction in A.D. 70], they forbade *the crowns of the bridegrooms* and the [wedding] drum. (Mishnah, *Sotah* 9:14)

In the war against Vespasian they decreed concerning *the wearing of wreaths by bridegrooms*. And what are the sort of bridegroom's wreaths [against which they decreed]? Those made of salt or brimstone. But those made of roses and myrtles they permitted. (Tosefta, *Sotah* 15:8)

Notice that both of these rabbinic writings depict the custom of crowning the bridegroom as being practiced in the first century A.D. Although neither text tells us exactly why the custom ceased, it is reasonable to assume that during the volatile years of the Jewish-Roman War (A.D. 66–70), any public symbol of royal identity—even a simple Jewish wedding crown—may have been considered politically dangerous. In any case, for our purposes, the way any first-century Jew would recognize the bridegroom was to look for the man wearing the crown. As Jewish scholar Michael Satlow puts it: the ancient Jewish bridegroom was "king for a day."

The same is true for Jesus, with one major difference. On one hand, like every other bridegroom in Jewish history, now that his wedding day has come, he too is dressed like a king and adorned with a crown. On the other hand, as the bridegroom of biblical prophecy, Jesus has come to be king not just for a day, or even a year, or even for forty years, but to reign forever over the everlasting kingdom of God. His marriage, just like his kingdom, is no ordinary marriage. His wedding crown is made of thorns and his wedding band is a rope, tied to the hard wood of a Roman cross.

The Seamless Garment of Jesus

In addition to describing the crowning of Jesus with thorns, the Gospels make a point of emphasizing another aspect of his clothing: the seamless garment for which the soldiers cast lots.

This garment is mentioned only in passing in the Gospels of Matthew and Mark, who refer to it after their accounts of the crowning with thorns:

> And when they had mocked him, they stripped him of the [royal] robe, and put his own clothes on him, and led him away to crucify him. (Matthew 27:31; cf. Mark 15:20)

As we have seen over and over in the course of this book, it is the Gospel of John that emphasizes the mystery of Jesus' identity as bridegroom. In his account of the fate of Jesus' garments, he tells us exactly what Jesus was wearing and what happened to his garments:

> When the soldiers had crucified Jesus they took his garments and made four parts, one for each soldier; also his tunic. *But the tunic was without seam, woven from top to bottom;* so they said to one another, "Let us not tear it, but cast lots for it to see whose it shall be." This was to fulfill the scripture, "They parted my garments among them, and for my clothing they cast lots." So the soldiers did this. (John 19:23–25)

From the perspective of the Roman soldiers, the act of casting lots for Jesus' "tunic" (Greek *chitōn*)—a long garment worn next to the skin—instead of tearing it into pieces is simple pragmatism. Somebody had to take possession of the condemned man's last piece of property in this world, and the seamless garment of Jesus would have been useless if it was torn apart.

The Jewish Bridegroom Is Dressed Like a Priest

However, when we look at the seamless garment of Jesus with the Jewish prophecies of the bridegroom in mind, something more is being revealed. Again, as any first-century Jew would have known, it was not only customary for the Jewish bridegroom to be crowned like a king. It was also customary for the bridegroom to be *dressed like a priest*.

In order to see this, it's important first to highlight how the "seamless garment" (Greek *chitōn araphos*) of Jesus is strikingly evocative of the "tunic" (Greek *chitōn*) worn by the ancient Jewish high priest. As both Jewish Scripture and tradition agree, one of the distinctive characteristics of the garments of the Jewish high priest was that they were not to be torn:

> "And you shall make the robe [of the high priest] all of blue. It shall have in it an opening for the head, with a woven binding around the opening ... *that it may not be torn*." (Exodus 28:31–32)

> *"The priest who is chief among his brethren*, upon whose head the anointing oil is poured, and *who has been consecrated to wear the garments, shall not ... rend his clothes*." (Leviticus 21:10)

> This vesture [of the high priest] was not composed of two pieces, nor was it sewed together upon the shoulders and the sides, *but it was one long vestment so wove as to have an aperture for the neck.* (Josephus, *Antiquities* 3.161)

In light of these parallels, a number of scholars conclude that the Gospel of John is highlighting the seemingly minor detail about Jesus' garment in order to reveal that Jesus is not just the Messiah but a priest. As New Testament scholar André Feuillet puts it: "For some, Jesus' seamless tunic recalls the likewise seamless robe of the high priest and means that the crucified Christ is a priest and his death a sacrifice he offers to God."

This connection between Jesus' garment and the priesthood is important for us because in ancient Judaism, *the bridegroom himself was dressed as a priest*. For example, both the Dead Sea Scrolls and the Targum interpret a passage from Isaiah with reference to the custom of a bridegroom dressing like a "priest" (Hebrew *kohen*) on his wedding day:

> I will greatly rejoice in the LORD, my soul shall exult in my God; for he has clothed me in the garments of salvation, he has covered me with the robe of righteousness, *as a bridegroom decks himself as a priest* (Hebrew *kohen*).... (1QIsaiah[a] 61:10)

> Jerusalem said, I will greatly rejoice in the Word of the LORD, my soul shall exult in the salvation of my God; for he has clothed me with garments of salvation, he has wrapped me with a robe of virtue, *as the bridegroom who prospers in his bride-chamber, and as the high priest who is prepared in his garments.... (Targum Isaiah 61:10)*

In light of such evidence, we can conclude that the ancient Jewish bridegroom was not only a symbolic "king for a day"; he was also a "priest for a day." To this day, in some Jewish circles the Jewish bridegroom continues to act as a kind of symbolic priest by dressing in the white priestly garment known in Hebrew as a *kitel* (perhaps from the Greek *chitōn*) on his wedding day.

The Bridegroom, the Bridechamber, and the Tabernacle

But why would the Jewish bridegroom be dressed like a priest? What was the significance of his wearing the same kind of garment a priest would wear while offering sacrifice in the Temple?

In order to answer this question, we need to remind ourselves of the symbolism of the Jewish bridechamber. As we saw earlier, according to ancient rabbinic tradition, the bridechamber into which the bridegroom and bride would enter on their wedding night was deliberately designed to resemble the Tabernacle of Moses. In the words of the ancient rabbis:

> If a man received it from his fellow to build him a *bridechamber* for his son . . . he must build it four cubits by six. . . . *The Sanctuary affords proof for this.* (Mishnah, *Baba Bathra* 6:4)

> As the bridal chamber is decorated with all kinds of colors, so was the Tabernacle decorated with all kinds of colors, "Blue, and purple, and scarlet, and fine linen" (Exodus 25:4), "That the spices thereof may flow" (Song 4:16). (*Numbers Rabbah* 13:12)

In other words, the bridechamber into which the Jewish bridegroom entered was evocative of the sanctuary, the supreme place of priestly sacrifice. From this point of view, a striking analogy is established between the union of God and Israel in the Tabernacle at Mount Sinai and the union of the Jewish bridegroom and his bride in the "tabernacle" of the "bridechamber" (Hebrew *huppah*). Just as God was united to his bride, Israel, through the covenant sacrifice in the Tabernacle of Moses, so too the Jewish bridegroom was united to his bride in the miniature tabernacle of the bridechamber, in a permanent and loving marriage "covenant" (Malachi 2:14).

The same is true of the Bridegroom Messiah. When the time comes for his wedding day on the cross, Jesus "decks himself as a priest" (1QIsaiah^a 61:10) in order to offer the nuptial sacrifice of his own flesh and blood, through which God will be united to his people in a new and everlasting covenant.

The Blood and Water Flow from Jesus' Side

The third and final connection between the crucifixion of Jesus and an ancient Jewish wedding day can be seen in the Gospel of John's momentous account of Jesus' last moments on the cross. Although we have already explored John's account of the water from the side of Jesus, we need to revisit this text one last time, focusing again on the soldier's act of piercing Jesus' side:

> After this Jesus, knowing that all was now finished, said (to fulfill the scripture), "I thirst." A bowl full of common wine stood there; so they put a sponge full of the common wine on hyssop and held it to his mouth. When Jesus had received the wine, he said, *"It is finished";* and he bowed his head and gave up his spirit. Since it was the day of Preparation, in order to prevent the bodies from remaining on the cross on the sabbath (for that sabbath was a high day), the Jews asked Pilate that their legs might be broken, and that they might be taken away. So the soldiers came and broke the legs of the first, and of the other who had been crucified with him; but when they came to Jesus and saw that he was already dead, they did not break his legs. *But one of the soldiers pierced his side with a spear, and at once there came out blood and water. He who saw it has borne witness—his testimony is true, and he knows that he tells the truth—that you also may believe.* (John 19:28–35)

Once again, on the level of ancient history, the piercing of Jesus' side is just one more example of the brutal efficiency of a Roman execution. In order to avoid offending the Jews by leaving the bodies of the dead to hang overnight on the sabbath—something contrary to the law of Moses (Deuteronomy 21:23)—the soldiers take it upon themselves to make sure all three of the crucified men are dead. (Given the fact that it was the Passover holiday, and Jerusalem was filled with hundreds of thousands of Jews, a flagrant violation of the Mosaic law during the festival could easily have led to a riot.) By smashing the legs of the two thieves with an iron mallet, known in Latin as a *crurifragium,* the soldiers make it impossible for the condemned men to keep themselves from asphyxiating. After this cruel act, the thieves' deaths would be both painful and rapid. (Such was the unhappy fate of the "good thief" as well as the bad one.) In the same way, one of the soldiers makes certain that Jesus is dead by piercing him through the heart with a long spear.

The First Bride Is Created from Adam's Side

When we look at the piercing of Jesus' side with ancient Jewish Scripture and tradition in mind, we can draw a parallel between the flow of blood and water from his side and the biblical account of God taking flesh from the side of Adam in the Garden of Eden:

> So the LORD God caused a deep sleep to fall upon the man, and while he slept took one of his ribs and closed up its place with flesh; and the rib which the LORD God had taken from the man he made into a woman and brought her to the man. Then the man said, "This at last is bone of my bones and flesh of my flesh; she shall be called Woman, because she was taken out of Man." Therefore a man

leaves his father and his mother and cleaves to his wife, and they become one flesh. (Genesis 2:21–24)

Although most English translations say that God created Eve from one of Adam's "ribs," the actual Hebrew text says that God took one of Adam's "sides" (Hebrew *tzela'*). Once this point is clear, we can see the similarities between the creation of Eve and the crucifixion of Jesus more easily. Just as Adam falls into a deep sleep so that God can create the Woman from his "side" (Hebrew *tzela'*; Greek *pleura*) (Genesis 2:21), so too Jesus falls into the sleep of death, and blood and water flow from his "side" (Greek *pleura*) (John 19:34). And just as the miraculous creation of the first bride from the side of Adam is the foundation for the marriage of man and woman, so too the miraculous flow of blood and water from the side of Jesus is the origin and foundation of the marriage of Christ and the Church. In the words of Saint Augustine, who recognized this parallel many centuries ago:

> [In] those two original humans . . . the marriage of Christ and the Church was prefigured. . . . [A]s Adam was a type of Christ, so too was the creation of Eve from the sleeping Adam a pre-figuration of the creation of the Church from the side of the Lord as he slept, for as he suffered and died on the cross and was struck by a lance, the sacraments which formed the Church flowed forth from him. By Christ's sleeping we are also to understand his passion. . . . *As Eve came from the side of the sleeping Adam, so the Church was born from the side of the suffering Christ.* (Augustine, *Exposition of the Psalms* 138:2)

In other words, just as Eve was given life by the miraculous gift of flesh from Adam, the first bridegroom, so too the Church—the bride of Jesus—receives her life through the twofold gift: the "living water" of the Holy Spirit that is given in baptism and the living "blood" of Jesus that is received in the Eucharist. And just as natural life was given to Eve, and, through Eve, to all humanity, through the flesh from the side of Adam, so supernatural life is given to the Church through the water and blood from the side of Jesus the Bridegroom.

The Apostle Paul and the "Great Mystery" of Jesus' Marriage

Should there be any doubt about this interpretation of Jesus' crucifixion as a recapitulation of the wedding of Adam and Eve, it's important to point out that it finds support in the writings of the apostle Paul. In his letter to the Ephesians, Paul not only describes the sacrificial death of Christ for the Church in terms of a husband's love for his wife; he also explicitly describes the love between Christ and the Church as a "great mystery," echoing the text about the wedding of Adam and Eve in the book of Genesis:

> Husbands, love your wives, *as Christ loved the church and gave himself up for her,* that he might sanctify her, having cleansed her by the washing of water with the word, that he might present the church to himself in splendor, without spot or wrinkle or any such thing, that she might be holy and without blemish. Even so husbands should love their wives as their own bodies. He who loves his wife loves himself. For no man ever hates his own flesh, but nourishes and cherishes it, as Christ does the church, because we are members of his body. *"For this reason a man shall leave his father and mother and be joined to his wife, and the two shall become one."* [Genesis 2:24]. *This is a great mystery, and I mean in reference to Christ and the church.* (Ephesians 5:25–32)

We will come back to this passage later when we look at the mystery of Christian marriage. For now the main point is this: the "great mystery" (Greek *mysterion mega*) to which Paul refers is the mystery of Christ's spousal love for the Church, which was manifested above all when he "loved her" (Greek *agapaō*) and "gave himself for her" on the cross. Thus the day of Jesus' crucifixion is his wedding day, when he, the new Adam, is "joined (Greek *proskollaō*) to his wife," the Church, in an everlasting marriage covenant.

In other words, Jesus is united with his bride through the sacrifice of his own flesh and blood, poured out literally on Calvary and then miraculously in the sacraments of the Church. In the words of Pope Benedict XVI:

> In this double outpouring of blood and water, the Fathers saw an image of two fundamental sacraments—Eucharist and Baptism—which spring forth from the Lord's pierced side, from his heart. *This is the new outpouring that creates the Church and renews mankind.* Moreover, the opened side of the Lord asleep on the Cross prompted the Fathers to point to the creation of Eve from the side of the sleeping Adam, and so in this outpouring of the sacraments they also recognized the birth of the Church: *the creation of the new woman from the side of the new Adam.*

5

The End of Time

We could stop there, at the foot of the cross, with the water and the blood flowing from the side of the new Adam. But as anyone who has ever been married knows, the wedding day is not the end but rather the *beginning* of the spousal relationship. "Till death do us part," as the saying goes (though in the case of Jesus and his bride it is "Through death we are joined").

The Bible, however, does not end with the cross. In the New Testament, the story of Jesus and his bride continues after the wedding ceremony. In an ordinary wedding, after the bride has prepared herself, the wedding banquet has been served, and the covenant sealed, the bridegroom takes the bride home to live with him. But when we turn to Jesus the Bridegroom, something very strange takes place. Not long after his wedding is inaugurated in the "hour" of his passion, death, and resurrection, he *leaves*. As the Gospels tell us, on the third day Jesus is raised from the dead and appears to his disciples (Matthew 28; Mark 16; Luke 24; John 21), and forty days later he ascends into heaven (Acts 1:1–11).

What do we make of this? What kind of bridegroom marries his bride and then (literally) "takes off"?

In order to answer this question, we need to recognize something extremely important: *although the wedding of the Messiah and his bride has begun, it is not yet fully complete.* This is easy to grasp if we remind ourselves that the bride of Jesus is not any individual human being but the entire people of God redeemed by his blood. And while billions and billions of people have been united to Jesus over the centuries through the water and blood that continue to flow from his cross in baptism and the Eucharist, there are still countless souls who have not yet been washed and not yet drunk the wine of salvation. Moreover, even those who have come to faith in the Bridegroom and become members of his bride have often "soiled" their wedding garments through sin and acts of spiritual infidelity. In other words, the great wedding of God and humanity is already underway, but not yet complete.

So when does the story end? How is the union of God and his people brought to its ultimate fulfillment? By this point in our study, the answer should be clear: just as the Jewish Bible *begins* with the marriage of Adam and Eve, the New Testament *ends* with the marriage of God and humanity in the great "wedding supper" at the end of time (Revelation 19:7). While many people think of the end of the world primarily (if not exclusively) as a time of tribulation, apostasy, deception, and the coming of the Antichrist, the New Testament also describes the end of time in another way: *as the eternal marriage of Jesus and his bride* in a "new heavens and a new earth" (Revelation 21:1–2). In this chapter, we will take a few moments to flesh out what it means for the Bible to end this way, and what light it sheds on the "great mystery" of Jesus' love for the Church.

THE BRIDEGROOM COMES BACK

The first hints that Jesus' marriage will not be completed until the end of time can be found by going back to his words to the disciples at the Last Supper. As we saw in chapter 2, in the words of institution Jesus speaks of the pouring out of his blood as establishing the new wedding covenant between God and the new Israel, represented by the twelve disciples (Matthew 26:26–28; Mark 14:22–25; Luke 22:19–20; 1 Corinthians 11:23–25). According to the Gospel of John, during the Last Supper Jesus also declares that he will leave his disciples behind. The reason: he is going to his Father's house to prepare a place for them, so that he can—at some undetermined point in the future—return and take them to be with him:

> "Let not your hearts be troubled; believe in God, believe also in me. In my Father's house are many rooms; if it were not so, would I have told you that I go to prepare a place for you? *And when I go and prepare a place for you, I will come again and will take you to myself, that where I am you may be also.*" (John 14:1–3)

At first glance it may seem as if these words are simply an elegant way for Jesus to say to his disciples: "Don't worry, I'll be back." Given that Jesus is at one and the same time the Messiah and the Bridegroom of Jewish prophecy, and his Last Supper is a wedding banquet of the new covenant, his telling the apostles that he goes to "prepare a place" for them takes on a new meaning when we compare it to ancient Jewish marriage customs.

The Jewish Bridegroom Prepares a Place for His Bride

In ancient Jewish tradition, one of the duties of the bridegroom was *to prepare a home for his bride,* so that when the wedding was finally consummated he could take her from her own family and bring her to live with him and be a part of his family in his father's house. As the modern Jewish scholar Schmuel Safrai says: "The groom would go out to receive the bride and bring her into his house; in fact the wedding ceremony was essentially the groom's introduction of the bride into his house." For example, according to one ancient Jewish tradition it was customary for a man to build a house before marrying his wife:

> The Torah has thus taught a rule of conduct: that *a man should build a house, plant a vineyard, and then marry a wife.* Similarly declared Solomon in his wisdom, "Prepare your work without, and make it ready for you in the field; and afterwards build your house" (Proverbs 24:27). *"Prepare your work without"*—*that is, a dwelling-place;* "and make it ready for you in the field"—*that is, a vineyard; "and afterwards build your house"*—*that is, a wife.* (Babylonian Talmud, *Sotah* 44a)

In contrast to modern-day weddings, in which the couple will often get married and then pool their resources in order to buy a home or apartment, in first-century Judaism, it was the duty of the bridegroom to go and prepare a place for his bride to dwell before he took her to himself. Indeed, this custom may explain how it was that Joseph and Mary the mother of Jesus were "betrothed" for some time before they came to dwell "together" as husband and wife (see Matthew 1:18, 25).

In light of this ancient Jewish background, New Testament scholar Adeline Fehribach suggests that in Jesus' words to his disciples regarding his going "to prepare a place" in his "Father's house" (John 14:2–3) we have another image of Jesus as Bridegroom. As she puts it:

> [T]he wedding ceremony in the first century was essentially the groom's induction of the bride into his house. . . . Thus, Jesus' words could have been viewed within the context of the messianic bridegroom taking his bride into his Father's house.

If this suggestion is correct, then it seems that at the Last Supper Jesus is explaining his imminent departure in a very Jewish way. Although he and the twelve disciples have celebrated the wedding feast of the new covenant, he must leave them for a time, in order to prepare the eternal "dwelling place" (Greek *topos*) into which he will one day bring his bride to be with him forever. Given all the connections we have seen so far between the marriage of God and Israel and worship in the Temple, it should come as no surprise that Jesus' image of his "Father's house" is recognized by many scholars as an allusion to the heavenly temple (cf. John 2:16–21).

From this point of view, Jesus' second coming at the end of time involves his coming not only "to judge the living and the dead" (as in the Apostle's Creed) and to destroy the works of the Antichrist (as in 2 Thessalonians 2), but also to *take his bride home with him* to dwell with him in the place he has prepared for her in the heavenly temple.

The Unexpected Return of the Bridegroom Messiah

In addition to the implicit comparison he makes at the Last Supper between his second coming and the return of the bridegroom, Jesus also explicitly compares his final advent to the belated and unexpected arrival of a Jewish bridegroom at his wedding:

[Jesus said:] "Then the kingdom of heaven shall be compared to ten virgins who took their lamps and went to meet the bridegroom. Five of them were foolish, and five were wise. For when the foolish took their lamps, they took no oil with them; but the wise took flasks of oil with their lamps. *As the bridegroom was delayed, they all slumbered and slept. But at midnight there was a cry, 'Behold, the bridegroom! Come out to meet him.'* Then all those virgins rose and trimmed their lamps. And the foolish said to the wise, 'Give us some of your oil, for our lamps are going out.' But the wise replied, 'Perhaps there will not be enough for us and for you; go rather to the dealers and buy for yourselves.' And while they went to buy, the bridegroom came, and those who were ready went in with him to the marriage feast; and the door was shut. Afterward the other maidens came also, saying, 'Lord, lord, open to us.' But he replied, 'Truly, I say to you, I do not know you.' Watch therefore, for you know neither the day nor the hour." (Matthew 25:1–13)

Although there is much that could be said about this parable, for our purposes the main point is simple. Jesus is describing the coming of the kingdom of God and the final judgment in terms of the unexpected return of "the bridegroom" (Greek *ho nymphios*) and the entry of the wedding guests into the joy of a great "marriage feast" (Greek *gamos*) (Matthew 25:10). Yet, as we found in our earlier explorations of the bridegroom theme in other parables of Jesus, there is always some kind of twist that reveals the deeper meaning.

On one hand, by comparing the coming of the kingdom of God to the arrival of a bridegroom, Jesus is drawing on customs associated with ancient wedding processions. Unlike modern-day weddings, which tend to climax with the *departure* of the bride and the groom for their honeymoon, ancient Jewish weddings climaxed with the *arrival* of the bridegroom at the wedding feast, when he came to take the bride to himself. For example, the book of Maccabees describes one bride coming with a large escort—presumably of virgin companions—and the bridegroom coming to meet her:

> The sons of Jambi are celebrating a great wedding, and are conducting the bride . . . with a large escort. . . . And the bridegroom came out with his friends and his brothers to meet them with tambourines and musicians and many weapons. (1 Maccabees 9:37, 39)

Along similar lines, a later rabbinic tradition establishes the coming of the bridegroom to meet his bride as a basic part of the Jewish wedding ceremony when it refers to "the time when the bridegroom goes out to meet his bride" (Babylonian Talmud, *Berakoth* 59b). In light of such evidence, it seems clear that in an ancient Jewish context, the procession of the bridegroom to meet his bride was a proverbial image of the joyful climax of a wedding celebration.

On the other hand, as with all the parables, there are several aspects of the parable of the ten virgins that don't fit in with our sense of what should happen at an ordinary wedding. For one thing, when the bridegroom finally does arrive, he is rather harsh toward the five virgins who ran out of oil. What kind of bridegroom would shut the door in the faces of the bridesmaids in his own wedding party? After all, it's not *their* fault he was late! And what kind of bridesmaids would be so unwilling to share their oil with their friends, and then be praised for doing so by Jesus in the parable?

Taken together, these kinds of extreme actions are important clues that this is no ordinary wedding banquet, this is no ordinary bridegroom, and these are no ordinary virgins. Instead, from an ancient Jewish perspective, the coming of the "bridegroom" (Greek *nymphios*) in the middle of the night refers to the unexpected advent of the Messiah at the final judgment (Matthew 25:6). The "marriage feast" (Greek *gamos*) is the eschatological banquet of the kingdom of heaven (Matthew 25:10). And the ten "maidens" or "virgins" (Greek *parthenoi*) represent two kinds of people: those who are spiritually prepared for the final judgment (the five who have enough "oil" for their lamps), and those who are spiritually unprepared (those whose "oil" runs out) (Matthew 25:8–9). As a result of their being ready to greet the bridegroom in joyful procession, the five wise virgins carry their lamps and are welcomed into the joy of the eternal kingdom of God. In the words of biblical commentator Cornelius A. Lapide: "The bridegroom is Christ, the bride is the Church, whose espousals take place in this life, but the eternal marriage shall be in the future glory of the resurrection."

THE WEDDING SUPPER OF THE LAMB

After the Gospel of John, there is no book of Scripture that is more attuned to the mystery of Jesus the Bridegroom than the book of Revelation, the Apocalypse of John. Although the book of Revelation is famous for its visions of wars, false prophets, bloodshed, and end-time horrors, the book does not climax with any of these events. Instead, according to Revelation, all of human history is headed toward the wedding supper of the Lamb and the unveiling of the bride of Christ. In a series of striking nuptial images, Revelation describes the coming of the kingdom at the end of time as follows:

> Hallelujah! For the Lord our God the Almighty reigns. Let us rejoice and exult and give him the glory, *for the marriage of the*

Lamb has come, and his Bride has made herself ready. . . . (Revelation
19:6–7)

Then I saw a new heaven and a new earth; for the first heaven
and the first earth had passed away, and the sea was no more.
*And I saw the holy city, new Jerusalem, coming down out of heaven
from God, prepared as a bride adorned for her husband;* and I heard
a great voice from the throne saying, "Behold, the dwelling of
God is with men. He will dwell with them, and they shall be his
people, and God himself will be with them; he will wipe away
every tear from their eyes, and death shall be no more, neither
shall there be mourning nor crying nor pain any more, for the
former things have passed away. . . ." (Revelation 21:1–4)

Here we have some of the most detailed descriptions in the Bible
of what is commonly known as "the end of the world." And how
does the book of Revelation describe the end? *As the eternal marriage
of the Messiah and "the Bride, the wife of the Lamb," the new Jerusalem.*

The True Meaning of "Apocalypse"

One reason this vision of the marriage at the end of time is so
striking is because it has the power to completely transform the
way we think of the Apocalypse. When most people say the word
"apocalypse" in English, they mean "the catastrophic destruction
of the universe"—that is, something really, really bad! However,
as several scholars have shown, in an ancient Jewish context the
Greek word *apokalypsis* has an often overlooked meaning. In the
words of Scott Hahn:

[Marriage] is also a symbol of a far greater mystery—the love
that Christ has for his bride, the Church, the love that God has

for His people. This mystery receives its most powerful expression in the last book of the Bible, the Revelation of Saint John, otherwise known as the Apocalypse—from the Greek word *apokalypsis,* which literally means "unveiling." Like the story of Adam and Eve, the Apocalypse evokes images that are both nuptial and priestly, for veils were then, as now, a standard part of a bride's wardrobe. *The bride's "unveiling"—apokalypsis—was the culmination of the Jews' traditional weeklong wedding feast.*

In other words, in this vision of the new Jerusalem, John is being given the privilege to see in advance what every eye will see at the end of time: the "unveiling" (Greek *apokalypsis*) of the bride of Christ. Just as an ancient Jewish bridegroom would lift the veil of his bride on their wedding day, so too at the end of time Jesus will unveil the glory of his bride, the new Jerusalem.

The Unveiling of the Bride of Jesus

Moreover, the book of Revelation not only describes the end of time as the "unveiling" of Jesus' bride; it actually goes on to tell you *exactly what she looks like.*

Everyone knows that the appearance of the bride is the climactic moment of the wedding ceremony. At that point in the service, everyone turns around or cranes their neck to catch a glimpse of her, even if they know her very well. So too when the angel shows the bride of Jesus to John, we look to see how she is adorned, and we immediately recognize that she is no *ordinary* bride. Although the description of the bride is lengthy, it is worth quoting here as fully as possible in order to try to "see" her through ancient Jewish eyes. If you've ever wondered what heaven "looks like," this is the closest thing to a guided tour that you will ever get:

Then came one of the seven angels . . . and spoke to me, saying, *"Come, I will show you the Bride, the wife of the Lamb."* And
in the Spirit he carried me away to a great, high mountain,
and showed me the holy city Jerusalem coming down out of
heaven from God, having the glory of God, its radiance like a
most rare jewel, like a jasper, clear as crystal. It had a great, high
wall, with twelve gates, and at the gates twelve angels, and on
the gates the names of the twelve tribes of the sons of Israel
were inscribed. . . . And the wall of the city had twelve foundations, and on them the twelve names of the twelve apostles of
the Lamb. . . . The city lies foursquare, its length the same as its
breadth; and he measured the city with his rod, twelve thousand
stadia [nearly fifteen hundred miles]; its length and breadth and
height are equal. . . . The wall was built of jasper, while the city
was pure gold, clear as glass. The foundations of the wall of the
city were adorned with every jewel; the first was jasper, the second sapphire, the third agate, the fourth emerald, the fifth onyx,
the sixth carnelian, the seventh chrysolite, the eighth beryl, the
ninth topaz, the tenth chrysoprase, the eleventh jacinth, the
twelfth amethyst. And the twelve gates were twelve pearls, each
of the gates made of a single pearl, and the street of the city was
pure gold, transparent as glass. And I saw no temple in the city,
for its temple is the Lord GOD the Almighty and the Lamb. . . .
(Revelation 21:9–12, 14, 16, 18–22)

What a strange-looking bride! Although a whole book could be
written on John's description of the new Jerusalem, for our purposes here, four features of the unveiled bride of Christ stand out
as important from an ancient Jewish perspective.

The New Jerusalem

First, the bride in the book of Revelation is a *new Jerusalem*. As we saw in earlier chapters, the city of Jerusalem was often identified by the prophets as the bride of God. Unlike the Jerusalem of the prophets who was an "adulterous" wife, there is "nothing unclean" about this new Jerusalem (Revelation 21:27). Here then we have at last the fulfillment of Isaiah's prophecy:

> For Zion's sake I will not keep silent, and for Jerusalem's sake I will not rest . . . You shall be a crown of beauty in the hand of the LORD, and a royal diadem in the hand of your God. You shall no more be termed Forsaken, and your land shall no more be termed Desolate; but you shall be called My delight is in her, and your land Married; for the LORD delights in you, and your land shall be married. . . . *As the bridegroom rejoices over the bride, so shall your God rejoice over you*. . . . (Isaiah 62:1, 3–5)

When the book of Revelation is interpreted in light of Jewish Scripture, the new Jerusalem is revealed as nothing less than the bride of God—a bride so intimately united to the Lord that her "new name" is "Married" (Hebrew *Beulah*). Note that well: the name of the bride of Jesus is not like the names of other nations—it is not "America" (the land of "Amerigo Vespucci"), or "Europe" (the land of "wide gazing"), or "Asia" (the land of Asia', the wife of Prometheus). It is *Beulah* land—the "Married" land—because in its deepest mystery it is the land where the God of the universe is united to his people in a covenant of love forever.

The New Israel

Second, the bride of the Lamb is also a *new Israel*. On one hand, she embodies the people of the old covenant through the symbols of the "twelve gates" and the "twelve tribes of the sons of Israel" (Revelation 21:12). On the other hand, she is built on the foundation of the "twelve apostles of the Lamb" (Revelation 21:12–14).

Perhaps the most powerful of all these images of the new Israel is John's description of the bride of Jesus as being adorned with twelve kinds of jewels: jasper, sapphire, agate, and so on (Revelation 21:19–20). As any first-century Jew would have recognized, this is not just a random set of jewels. The Bride of Jesus is covered with *the twelve jewels worn by the Jewish high priest when offering sacrifice in the Tabernacle,* jewels symbolizing the twelve tribes of Israel:

> [God said to Moses:] "And you shall make a breastpiece of judgment ... And you shall set in it four rows of stones.... There shall be twelve stones with their names according to the names of the sons of Israel; they shall be like signets, each engraved with its name, for the twelve tribes.... *So Aaron shall bear the names of the sons of Israel in the breastpiece of judgment upon his heart, when he goes into the holy place, to bring them to continual remembrance before the LORD.* ... And they shall be upon Aaron's heart, when he goes in before the LORD; thus Aaron shall bear the judgment of the people of Israel upon his heart before the LORD continually. (Exodus 28:15, 17, 21, 29–30)

Once we juxtapose John's vision of the bride of the Lamb with this description of the stones that adorn the breastpiece of the priest Aaron, the meaning of the precious stones on the foundation wall of the heavenly city suddenly becomes very clear. The twelve stones adorning the new Jerusalem represent *the souls of the chosen people of God,* who are like precious jewels in the eyes of God. Just as the ancient high priest would bear the jewels representing the twelve tribes of Israel "upon his heart" when he entered into God's presence in the holy of holies, so now Jesus, the true High Priest, bears the souls of the new people of God "upon his heart" as he brings them into the eternal city of God. The Spirit unveils for John (and for us) how Jesus the Bridegroom sees the souls of the people of God: as precious gems, holy and beautiful in his eyes, and always close to his heart.

The New Temple

Third, the bride of Jesus is also a *new temple.* That is the meaning of the shape of the city, which is described as "foursquare," or a cube (Revelation 21:16). As any ancient Jew familiar with the Scriptures would have recognized, the perfectly cubical shape of the new Jerusalem is modeled on the golden cube of the holy of holies:

> The inner sanctuary [King Solomon] prepared in the innermost part of the house, to set there the ark of the covenant of the LORD. *The inner sanctuary was twenty cubits long, twenty cubits wide, and twenty cubits high; and he overlaid it with pure gold.* (1 Kings 6:19–20)

As John goes on to say, there is no separate temple in the new Jerusalem, because "its temple is the Lord God the Almighty and the Lamb" (Revelation 21:22). In other words, in the new Jerusalem there is no longer any division or separation between God and his people. All this has been overcome, so that the city is a "living temple" of God.

The New Eden

Fourth and finally, the bride of Jesus is depicted as a *new Eden*. Although this feature of the bride may not be clear from the description we've seen thus far from the book of Revelation, it becomes clear when the angel shows John the "interior" of the new Jerusalem:

> Then he showed me *the river of the water of life,* bright as crystal, flowing from the throne of God and of the Lamb through the middle of the street of the city; also, on either side of the river, *the tree of life* with its twelve kinds of fruit, yielding its fruit each month; and the leaves of the tree were for the healing of the nations. There shall no more be anything accursed, but the throne of God and of the Lamb shall be in it, and his servants shall worship him; *they shall see his face,* and his name shall be on their foreheads. And night shall be no more; they need no light of lamp or sun, for the Lord God will be their light, and they shall reign for ever and ever. (Revelation 22:1–5)

With these words, the divine love story of salvation history comes full circle. Just as the Bible begins with the "wedding" of Adam and Eve in the Garden of Eden, watered by four rivers (Genesis 2–3), so now the Bible ends with the wedding of Jesus the Bridegroom and the Church, his bride, in a new Eden watered by the supernatural "river of life." This is the deepest mystery of the end of time: the eternal marriage of God and his people in Christ and the new Jerusalem, so that human beings will at last be able to *see the face of God,* which is the face of the divine Bridegroom.

NO MARRIAGE IN THE RESURRECTION?

With all of this in mind, before we bring this chapter to a close, there is one last text that we have to deal with. How do we reconcile the eternal wedding of Jesus and his bride in the new creation with Jesus' well-known (and, for many, disturbing) teaching that there will be *no marriage* in the resurrection?

In order to answer this question, we need to take a moment to look carefully at what Jesus had to say about this issue and try to understand it too in its ancient Jewish context.

The Question About Marriage in the Resurrection

According to the Gospel accounts of his life, on one occasion during his public ministry Jesus was questioned by the Sadducees about whether or not there would be any marriage in the resurrection. Although the episode is recorded in all three Synoptic Gospels (Matthew 22:23–33; Mark 12:18–27; Luke 20:27–38), for the sake of space we will focus on the account in the Gospel of Mark, the first half of which states:

> And Sadducees came to him, who say that there is no resurrection; and they asked him a question, saying, "Teacher, Moses wrote for us that if a man's brother dies and leaves a wife, but leaves no child, the man must take the wife, and raise up children for his brother. There were seven brothers; the first took a wife, and when he died left no children; and the second took her, and died, leaving no children; and the third likewise; and the seven left no children. Last of all the woman also died. In the resurrection whose wife will she be? For the seven had her as wife." (Mark 12:18–23)

In order to understand the question put to Jesus by the Sadducees, a few facts about ancient Judaism are in order.

For one thing, in the first century A.D., most Jews believed in
the immortality of the soul after death and the resurrection of the
body at the end of time. This bodily form of afterlife is what both
Jesus and the Sadducees are referring to when they speak about
"the resurrection" (Greek *anastasis*) (Mark 12:18). The Sadducees
in the time of Jesus were among the elite of Jerusalem, and they
were known for not believing in the bodily resurrection of the
dead at the end of time, nor in the immortality of the soul. Thus,
the question they put to Jesus about marriage in the resurrection
is not entirely honest. Indeed, they are seeking to make the idea
of the resurrection ridiculous by imagining a scenario in which
a Jewish woman who had been married multiple times would
find herself wed to seven husbands. The reason this scenario was
even a possibility was because of what is known as the law of
levirate marriage (from the Latin *laevus vir,* meaning "brother-in-
law"). According to the Torah, if a man died childless, it was the
duty of his brother to take his widow as a wife and have children
with her, thereby providing heirs who would carry on the dead
brother's name and inheritance. With this law as a given, the Sadducees are trying to trap Jesus into either rejecting the Torah or
proposing the morally problematic picture of a bodily resurrection in which one woman would act as the wife of seven men at
one time!

As is so often the case in the Gospels, not only does Jesus
avoid the trap set by his opponents; he also uses the occasion to
teach something about the kingdom of God. In this case, he turns
the Sadducees' mockery around on them, taking the opportunity
to show how ignorant they are of the true nature of the resurrection, in which there will *be* no marriage:

Jesus said to them, "Is not this why you are wrong, that you know neither the scriptures nor the power of God? *For when they rise from the dead, they neither marry nor are given in marriage, but are like angels in heaven.* And as for the dead being raised, have you not read in the book of Moses, in the passage about the bush, how God said to him, 'I am the God of Abraham, and the God of Isaac, and the God of Jacob'? He is not God of the dead, but of the living; you are quite wrong." (Mark 12:24–27)

What is the meaning of these mysterious words? Given everything we have seen over the course of this book about the importance of marital imagery in Jewish Scripture, how can Jesus say that there will be no marriage in the resurrection? Does this mean that husbands and wives will no longer know each other? Is there something wrong with marriage that it must pass away in the world to come? And what does Jesus mean by saying that men and women in the resurrection will be "like the angels"?

There are at least two key reasons for Jesus' otherwise puzzling decree that there will be no marriage in the resurrection, and these can be explained by ancient Jewish beliefs.

After the Bodily Resurrection, There Will Be No More Death

First, after the bodily resurrection of the dead at the end of time, there will be no more death. In the Gospel of Luke's account, Jesus makes this point explicit when he says:

"The sons of this age marry and are given in marriage; but those who are accounted worthy to attain to that age and to the resurrection from the dead neither marry nor are given in marriage, *for they cannot die any more,* because they are equal

to angels and are sons of God, being sons of the resurrection."
(Luke 20:34–36)

Contrary to the popular (and completely unbiblical) idea that
human beings *become* angels after death, Jesus here makes quite clear
that men and women in the resurrection will be "like angels" (Mark
12:25) or "equal to angels" (Luke 20:36) because they will be immortal. Presumably, then, Jesus is assuming that one of the primary
reasons for earthly marriage is procreation, in order to continue the
human race. After the resurrection, death will be no more, so there
will no longer be any need for offspring. Earthly marriage, bound
up as it is with the overcoming of death through procreation, is a
temporary part of "this age" or "this world" (Greek *aiōn*); it will
have no place in "that age," the age of the bodily resurrection.

Celibacy and the World to Come in Jewish Tradition

Second, and perhaps even more important, Jesus' declaration that
there will be no marriage after the resurrection of the body also
appears to reflect an ancient Jewish tradition that in the resurrection there will be no sexual relations.

As scholars have noted, this ancient tradition is extremely important for putting Jesus' response to the Sadducees in context.
Despite the fact that the ancient Jewish rabbis widely regarded
marriage and procreation as God-given gifts to the human race,
some of them also affirmed that in the future age, which they
called "the world to come," there would be no marriage or sexual relations. Compare the following rabbinic traditions with the
teaching of Jesus:

> In the future world there is no eating nor drinking *nor propaga-*
> *tion* ... but the righteous sit with their crowns on their heads

feasting on the brightness of the divine presence [Hebrew *shek-inah*], as it says, "And they beheld God, and did eat and drink" (Exodus 24:11). (Babylonian Talmud, *Berakoth* 17a)

In the World to Come sexual intercourse will be entirely for-bidden.... On that day that the Holy One, blessed be He, revealed Himself on Mount Sinai to give the Torah to the chil-dren of Israel, He forbade intercourse for three days, as it is said, "Be ready on the third day; do not go near a woman" [Exodus 19:15]. Now since God, when He revealed himself for only one day, forbade intercourse for three days, in the World-to-Come, when the presence of God [Hebrew *shekinah*] dwells continuously in Israel's midst, will not intercourse be entirely forbidden? (*Midrash on Psalms* 146:4)

Notice three striking aspects of these rabbinic teachings. First, both texts reflect the same idea we find in the teaching of Jesus: in the future world there will be no marital relations. Intriguingly, the rabbis even use the same expression as Jesus in the Gospel of Luke, speaking of "the world to come" or "the age to come" (Hebrew *ha 'olam haba'*). Second, marital relations in the "World to Come" will *not* cease because there is anything bad about mar-riage or procreation. From an ancient Jewish perspective, mar-riage and procreation were ordained by God at the beginning of the creation of this world: "Be fruitful and multiply, and fill the earth and subdue it" (Genesis 1:28). Instead, marriage and procre-ation pass away because they belong to "this world" (Hebrew, *ha 'olam hazeh*), which will itself eventually pass away.

Third and finally, both rabbinic teachings base their belief in the celibacy of the world to come on *the Israelites' abstinence from marital relations at Mount Sinai*. Although the point is often over-looked, according to the book of Exodus, God commanded the

Israelites to abstain from intercourse for three days in order to prepare to come into his presence on the mountain. "[Moses] said to the people, 'Be ready by the third day; do not go near a woman'" (Exodus 19:15). In fact, from that point forward, anytime the priests in the Temple went into the presence of God, they were likewise required to abstain (see 1 Samuel 21:1–6). As the rabbinic writings make abundantly clear, in the world to come, by definition, everyone will be in the presence of God *forever;* therefore, there will be no more marital relations between husband and wife.

The Eternal Marriage of the Lamb

Before closing, we can go one step further. Given everything we have seen so far about the eternal marriage of God and his people, I think that it is also possible to reformulate Jesus' teaching positively. The reason there will be no earthly marriage between men and women in the resurrection is not because all marriage will cease to exist, but because all of redeemed humanity will be married to God.

According to the book of Revelation, the glory of the kingdom of God will not mean the *absence* of all marriage, but the *fulfillment* of earthly marriage in the great wedding of Christ and the Church:

> Then I heard what seemed to be the voice of a great multitude, like the sound of many waters and like the sound of mighty thunderpeals, crying, "Hallelujah! For the Lord our God the Almighty reigns. Let us rejoice and exult and give him the glory, *for the wedding of the Lamb has come, and his Bride has made herself ready; it was granted her to be clothed with fine linen, bright and pure*"—for the fine linen is the righteous deeds of the saints.

And the angel said to me, "Write this: *Blessed are those who are invited to the wedding supper of the Lamb*." (Revelation 19:6–9)

Once this piece of the puzzle is put into place, we find that there is no opposition between the idea that there is no marriage in the resurrection and the idea that Jesus is the Bridegroom. Rather, we find that the one idea provides the explanation for the other. The *reason* there will be no ordinary earthly marriage in the bodily resurrection is that ordinary earthly marriage is a *sign* that points beyond itself to the *true* marriage: the union of Christ and the Church. Once the reality of the eternal marriage of God and his people in Christ has been fulfilled, there will no longer be any need for the earthly sign. In the life of the world to come, the goal of all marriage—personal communion and the gift of life—will be completely fulfilled by the union of the bride with Christ and his gift to her of eternal life.

6

The Bridal Mysteries

In my book *Jesus and the Jewish Roots of the Eucharist,* I told the story of traveling around the country and repeatedly being asked: *"Why haven't I ever heard this before?"* In more recent years, as I have begun to speak about Jesus the Bridegroom, I find myself getting asked the exact same question. On one recent occasion, after I had just given a lecture on Jesus and the Samaritan woman at the well, a woman came up to me and said: "I have been a Christian for sixty years, and I've never heard anything like this. Why?"

Well, to be frank, I don't know why. As a result, when I'm asked this question, it's always difficult to figure out exactly how to respond. One thing I always try to stress is that whatever the reason, it is certainly *not* because the idea is unimportant in the New Testament, ancient Christian writings, or contemporary Church teaching. To the contrary, from the very beginning the "great mystery" (Greek *mysterion mega*) of Christ's spousal love for the Church has stood not at the periphery of the Christian gospel but at the very center (Ephesians 5:32).

Indeed, over and over again, as you read the writings of the ancient Church Fathers, such as Cyril of Jerusalem, Augustine of Hippo, Ambrose, John Chrysostom, and many others, the theme of Christ's identity as Bridegroom and the Church's identity as bride is treated as a *staple* of Christian teaching. This basic insight is used to shed light on virtually every aspect of the Christian life, from its beginnings in baptism, to its sustenance in the Eucharist, to the various states of life, such as marriage and virginity. In more recent times, the contemporary *Catechism of the Catholic Church* sums up the importance of this mystery when it teaches:

> The nuptial covenant between God and his people Israel had prepared the way for the new and everlasting covenant in which the Son of God, by becoming incarnate and giving his life, has united to himself in a certain way all mankind saved by him, thus preparing for "the wedding feast of the Lamb." (CCC 1612)

> The entire Christian life bears the mark of the spousal love of Christ and the Church. (CCC 1617)

If this is true—if the *entire* Christian life is marked by the "spousal love" of Jesus for the Church—then our focus on Jesus the Bridegroom should have the power to shed light on not only the deeper meaning of his life and death on the cross, but also the deeper significance of what it means to be Christian.

In this chapter, I want to take a few moments to look at certain aspects of the Christian faith through the lens of Jesus' spousal love for the Church. For the sake of focus, we will limit ourselves to four mysteries of the Christian life that stand out in ancient and modern Christian writings as visible signs of the spousal relationship between Christ and the Church: baptism, the Eucharist, marriage, and consecrated virginity. As I hope to show, while the ideas we have been exploring in this book may be surprising for some readers, they are nothing new. They are part and parcel of what Christians have always believed about the "great mystery," and what the Church teaches to this very day.

BAPTISM

For many Christians, baptism is primarily an outward, public sign of inward repentance from sin. Think here of John the Baptist's call to his fellow Jews to receive his "baptism of repentance for the forgiveness of sins" (Mark 1:4). For others it is an ordinance of Jesus, a ritual to be performed because of the Great Commission: "Go therefore and make disciples of all nations, baptizing them in the name of the Father and of the Son and of the Holy Spirit" (Matthew 28:19). For many others, baptism is primarily a rite of initiation into the Christian community, by which a person becomes a member of the "one body" of Christ (1 Corinthians 12:13).

However, when we look at the mystery of baptism in the light of everything we've learned about Jesus the Bridegroom, another meaning emerges. If Jesus is the Bridegroom and the Church is his bride, then Christian baptism is more than just a sign of repentance, an ordinance, or a ritual of initiation; *it is the bridal bath by which Jesus cleanses us from sin so that we can be united to God.*

Baptism as a Bridal Bath in Ancient Christianity

The first hints of this understanding of baptism come from the apostle Paul. In his letter to the Ephesians, while teaching husbands to love their wives as Christ loved the Church (more on this below), Paul alludes to the mystery of baptism when he says:

Husbands, love your wives, as Christ loved the church and gave himself up for her, that he might sanctify her, *having cleansed her by the washing of water with the word,* that he might present the Church to himself in splendor, without spot or wrinkle or any such thing, that she might be holy and without blemish. (Ephesians 5:25–27)

As commentators both ancient and modern agree, when Paul speaks here of Christ "cleansing" (Greek *katharisas*) the Church through "the washing of water," he is alluding to the ritual washing with water that he refers to elsewhere as "baptism" (Greek *baptisma*) (see Ephesians 4:5). With these words, Paul is describing baptism in terms of an ancient Jewish wedding custom. As New Testament scholar Peter Williamson puts it:

In both Jewish and Greek cultures of that time, the immediate cosmetic preparation of the bride included a bath with fragrant oils so that she could be as clean and as beautiful as possible. Baptism, Paul is saying, is the Church's bridal bath that prepares her to be united to her bridegroom.

Notice one key difference between this Jewish custom and the mystery of baptism. In an ordinary Jewish nuptial bath it was the bride herself or her attendants who would wash and anoint her. When the Church is washed with water, however, it is *the Bridegroom himself* who bathes his bride in the waters of baptism, so that she might be "holy" (Greek *hagios*) and cleansed from sin. Strikingly, in later Jewish tradition the betrothal of a Jewish bridegroom and bride actually came to be known as "making holy" or "consecration" (Hebrew *qiddushin*)—because the bride was "made holy" or "set apart" (Hebrew *qadosh*) for her husband.

Once this background is clear, we can see that for Paul, baptism is not just a ritual washing, but a mystery that flows from the passion and death of Jesus on the cross. As biblical scholar Andrew Lincoln puts it: "If Christ's death is the point in history at which his love was demonstrated, baptism is the point at which the Church experiences Christ's continuing purifying love for her as his bride." In other words, baptism is a nuptial mystery of the forgiving love of Jesus because its power to cleanse from sin flows directly from the nuptial mystery of the cross, when Jesus the Bridegroom poured out his love for the Church, a love that "covers a multitude of sins" (cf. 1 Peter 4:8).

Following the lead of Saint Paul, in the early centuries of the Church many of the Church Fathers discussed the mystery of baptism in terms of the bridal bath. Perhaps the most memorable use of this image comes from the writings of Saint Cyril. In his lectures given during Lent to Christian converts about to be baptized, he describes baptism in this way:

> When you hear the texts from Scriptures concerning *the mysteries* [the sacraments], then you will have a spiritual perception of things once beyond your ken.... If it were your wedding day that was fixed, would you not, ignoring everything else, be wholly engaged in preparations for the marriage feast? *Then, on the eve of consecrating your soul to your heavenly Spouse, will you not put by the things of the body to win those of the spirit?* (Cyril of Jerusalem, *Protocatechesis* 1:6)

In other words, from an ancient Christian perspective, the preparation of converts for baptism was nothing less than a preparation for their "wedding day," in which they would be cleansed from sin and united to Jesus the Bridegroom.

The Baptismal Wedding Garment

Even more striking, in the ancient Christian Church it was a common custom for converts (known as catechumens) to disrobe just before being baptized. After baptism they would be dressed in a new white garment. (The custom of giving the baptized a white garment continues in many Christian circles to this day.)

According to several early Church Fathers the practice of disrobing at baptism was an outward symbol interpreted as the spiritual fulfillment of the disrobing of the bride in the Song of Solomon. As we recall from chapter 1, the earliest Christians followed ancient Jews in interpreting the Song of Songs as an allegory of God's love for his people. With this in mind, consider Cyril of Jerusalem's explanation for fourth-century converts of the baptismal disrobing and dressing in a new garment:

> Immediately, then, upon entering [the waters of baptism], you removed your garment. This was a figure of "stripping off the old man with his deeds" (Colossians 3:9). Having stripped, you were naked, in this also imitating Christ, who was naked on the cross. . . . *May the soul that has once put off that old self never again put it on, but say with the Bride in the Song of Songs: "I have put off my garment: how shall I put it on?"* (Song 5:3). You were naked in the sight of all and were not ashamed. Truly you bore the image of the first-formed Adam, who was naked in the garden and "not ashamed" (Genesis 2:25). (Cyril of Jerusalem, *Mystagogical Catechesis* 2:2)

In other words, from an ancient Christian perspective, the bride in the Song of Songs who disrobes, bathes, and is dressed in her bridal garment before being wed to her bridegroom is analogous to the candidate for baptism who is cleansed by the waters of the baptismal font, clothed in new garments, and united to Christ the Bridegroom. From this point of view, the new garment given in baptism is a *bridal garment,* symbolizing the fact that the baptized person has now become part of the bride of Christ, and, like Adam and Eve in the Garden of Eden, a new creation, free from sin.

The Beauty of the Baptized

Finally, for the early Church Fathers, because baptism is a nuptial bath, not only does it cleanse the baptized person from sin; it also makes him or her beautiful in Jesus' eyes. Once again, Saint Cyril of Jerusalem applies excerpts about the bride from the Song of Songs to describe what happens in the newly baptized:

> [The Lord] will pour upon you clean water and you shall be cleansed from all your sins. Choiring angels shall encircle you, chanting [from the Song of Songs:] "Who is that comes up all white and leaning upon her beloved?" [Song 8:5]. For the soul that was formerly a slave has now accounted her Lord as her kinsman, and He ... will answer: *"Ah, you are beautiful my beloved, ah, you are beautiful!"* [Song 4:1]. (Cyril of Jerusalem, *Catechesis* 3:16)

In light of these and many other texts from the Church Fathers describing baptism in this way, the great patristic scholar Jean Daniélou concludes that for the ancient Christian Church, "Baptism is seen in its fullness as a nuptial mystery. The soul, until now a simple creature, becomes the Bride of Christ. When she comes out of the baptismal water in which He has purified her in His Blood, He welcomes her in her white bridal robe and receives the promise which binds her to Him forever."

Baptism and the Spousal Love of Jesus

Significantly, this understanding of baptism is not something confined to the writings of the apostle Paul or the theology of a few early Church Fathers. It continues to be part of the official teaching of the Catholic Church today. For example, in one of his reflections on Paul's letter to the Ephesians, Pope John Paul II had this to say about the mystery of baptism:

> *The one who receives Baptism becomes at the same time—by virtue of the redemptive love of Christ—a participant in his spousal love for the Church.* "The washing of water accompanied by the word" (Ephesians 5:26) is ... the expression of spousal love in the sense that it prepares the Bride (the Church) for the Bridegroom, it makes the Church the Bride of Christ.... The same Bridegroom, Christ, takes care to adorn the Bride, the Church, in order that she might be beautiful with the beauty of grace, beautiful in virtue of the gift of salvation in its fullness, already granted from the moment of the sacrament of Baptism. (Pope John Paul II, *Man and Woman He Created Them*, 91:7)

Notice once again that John Paul II is pointing out that baptism is about more than the forgiveness of sins. It is a sacrament of *intimate union* with Jesus, through which the individual believer becomes part of the Mystical Body of all believers, the Church. The pope is also emphasizing that baptism is the sacramental expression of the "spousal love" of Jesus, which he manifested on the cross. This means that the cleansing with water is more than just a memorial of Jesus' own baptism in the Jordan River; *baptism is the way that Jesus communicates his love as bridegroom to each human person.* By means of this bridal bath, the human soul is washed in the river of "living water" that flowed from the side of the crucified

Bridegroom, and that soul is given the "spirit" that Christ handed over in his dying breath on the cross (John 7:37–39; 19:30).

The Bath Before the Wedding Banquet

From this point of view, baptism is not the end of the individual Christian's relationship with Jesus the Bridegroom but only the beginning. In one of the most beautiful lines from the *Catechism of the Catholic Church,* we read:

> Baptism, the entry into the People of God, is a nuptial mystery; it is so to speak *the nuptial bath which precedes the wedding feast,* the Eucharist. (CCC 1617)

In other words, one of the primary purposes of baptism is to prepare Christians for an even more intimate union with Jesus, which is achieved through participation in another nuptial mystery—the mystery of the Lord's Supper.

THE EUCHARIST

When we turn to the mystery of the Lord's Supper, also known as the Eucharist, we find the same kind of diversity of meaning that we did with baptism. For many Christians the Lord's Supper is primarily a "memorial" of the Last Supper and the events of the night on which Jesus was betrayed. As Jesus says: "Do this in remembrance of me" (Luke 22:19; 1 Corinthians 11:24–25). For others, it is a banquet of "thanksgiving" (Greek *eucharistia*) offered to God in gratitude for the gift of salvation, in union with Jesus, who "gave thanks" (Greek *eucharistēsas*) over the bread and wine before he died (Matthew 26:27; Mark 14:23). For still others, the Eucharist is primarily a sacrifice, in which the bloody sacrifice of the cross is made present through the unbloody offering of bread and wine, as described by the apostle Paul: "The cup of blessing which we bless, is it not a participation in the blood of Christ? The bread which we break, is it not a participation in the body of Christ?" (1 Corinthians 10:16).

However, when we look at the mystery of the Eucharist through the lens of Jesus' passion and death as the Bridegroom Messiah, another meaning comes to light. If Jesus is the Bridegroom and the Church is his bride, the Lord's Supper is not just a memorial, or a banquet of "thanksgiving," or a sacrifice; it is also *a wedding banquet* in which Jesus gives himself entirely to his bride in a new and everlasting marriage covenant.

The Wedding Supper of the Lamb

One doesn't have to look very hard or long to find abundant evidence in ancient Christianity for the understanding of the Eucharist as the wedding banquet of Christ and the Church.

As we've already seen, there are hints of just such an understanding in the book of Revelation's description of a heavenly "wedding banquet" to which the disciples of Jesus are invited:

> "Let us rejoice and exult and give him the glory, for *the wedding of the Lamb has come, and his Bride has made herself ready; it was granted her to be clothed with fine linen, bright and pure*"—for the fine linen is the righteous deeds of the saints. And the angel said to me, "Write this: *Blessed are those who are invited to the wedding supper of the Lamb*." (Revelation 19:7–9)

As we have seen earlier, on one hand, the wedding supper described here is a representation of the heavenly kingdom of God and the end of time. On the other hand, it is also an allusion to the wedding banquet of the Eucharist, to which Christians on earth (known as the "saints") are invited. As theologian Roch Kereszty writes: *"The eucharistic connotation of the wedding feast . . . is hard to miss.* Already in the 50s in his first letter to the Corinthians Paul uses the phrase *deipnon kuriakon* [Greek for "supper of the Lord"] to designate the Eucharist." In other words, the book of Revelation is deliberately describing the heavenly banquet of the kingdom of God in terms that are evocative of the Lord's Supper, to which Christians are invited and for which they should prepare themselves. This supper is both a participation in heavenly glory and an anticipation of the eternal marriage that will be fulfilled at the end of time.

Indeed, following in the footsteps of the book of Revelation, Saint Augustine writes that every celebration of the Eucharist is a renewal of the wedding of Christ and the Church:

> *Every Celebration [of the Eucharist] is a celebration of Marriage; the Church's nuptials are celebrated.* The King's Son is about to marry a wife, and the King's Son [is] himself a King; and the guests frequenting the marriage are themselves the Bride. . . . For all the Church is Christ's Bride, of which the beginning and first-fruits is the Flesh of Christ, because there was the Bride joined to the Bridegroom in the flesh. (Augustine, *Homilies on 1 John* 2:12–17)

In other words, in the Eucharistic "marriage celebration" (Latin *nuptiarum celebratio*), Jesus the Bridegroom is united to the Church, not just in spirit, but in body as well. For while Jesus, as the divine Son of God, is *spiritually* present everywhere, in the Eucharist he is present *bodily:* it is the wedding banquet at which the Bridegroom Messiah is united to his bride in both body and spirit.

The Eucharist and the "Kiss" of Christ

In a striking illustration of this mysterious union, Saint Ambrose, the fourth-century bishop of Milan, describes the Lord's Supper as the fulfillment of the "kiss" shared by the bridegroom and the bride in the Song of Songs. In one of his sermons to newly baptized Christians, Ambrose declares:

> You have come to the altar, the Lord Jesus calls you, for the text speaks of you or of the Church, and he says to you: "Let him kiss me with kisses of his mouth" [Song of Songs 1:1]. This word can be applied equally to Christ or to you. Do you wish to apply it to Christ? You see that you are pure from all sin, since your faults have been blotted out. This is why He judges you to be worthy of heavenly sacraments and invites you to the heavenly banquet: "May he kiss me with the kiss of his mouth" [Song of Songs 1:1]. You wish to apply the same to yourself? Seeing yourself pure from all sins and worthy to come to the altar of Christ.... *You see the wonderful sacrament and you say: "May he kiss me with the kiss of his mouth," that is, may Christ give me a kiss.* (Ambrose, *On the Sacraments,* 5:5–7)

What a grand vision of the Lord's Supper! This is especially so when we recall the ancient Jewish interpretation of the Song of Songs as an allegory of the love of God for Israel as expressed through *worship* in the Temple. In the words of Jean Daniélou, for the Church Fathers, the Eucharist was nothing less than "the kiss given by Christ to the soul, the expression of the union of love." In this way, the Eucharist fulfills the longing of bridal Israel for union with her God.

There is, however, a dark side to the mystery of the eucharistic kiss. Saint John Chrysostom, the fourth-century bishop of Constantinople, uses the very same image to warn against receiving the Lord's Supper in a state of unrepented grave sin. In Eucharistic liturgy composed by Chrysostom, the Christian faithful pray these striking words:

> O Son of God, bring me into communion today with your mystical supper. *I shall not tell your enemies the secret, nor kiss you with Judas' kiss.* But like the good thief I cry, "Jesus, remember me when you come into your kingdom." (CCC 1386)

For the early Church Fathers, knowingly receiving the Eucharist in a state of grave sin is like recapitulating the "kiss" of betrayal given by Judas to Jesus in the Garden of Gethsemane (Luke 22:47–48). Here again, sin is not just about breaking rules; it is the betrayal of a relationship.

The Eucharist as Jesus' Gift of Himself to His Bride

As with baptism, the idea of the Eucharist as a wedding banquet is not something confined to the writings of ancient mystics or a few Church fathers. It too is part of the official teaching of the Catholic Church today.

Once again, Pope John Paul II brings this aspect to the fore when he teaches that in the Eucharist Jesus gives his bride the wedding gift of himself:

> [With the Eucharist,] we find ourselves at the very heart of the Paschal Mystery, which completely reveals the spousal love of God. Christ is the Bridegroom because "he has given himself": his body has been "given," his blood has been "poured out" (cf. Luke 22:19–20). In this way "he loved them to the end" (John 13:1). *The "sincere gift" contained in the Sacrifice of the Cross gives*

definitive prominence to the spousal meaning of God's love. . . . The Eucharist is the Sacrament of our Redemption. It is the Sacrament of the Bridegroom and of the Bride. (John Paul II, Apostolic Letter On the Dignity and Vocation of Women [*Mulieris Dignitatem*], no. 26)

How many people today think of the Eucharist in this way, as "the Sacrament of the Bridegroom and the Bride"? Yet if love is defined as *the gift of oneself* to another person, then the Eucharist is the highest possible expression of Jesus' spousal love for the Church. In the Eucharist Jesus not only *tells* the Church he loves her; he *shows* his love by really and truly giving himself to her, in both body and spirit, as the divine Bridegroom. Note well that this kind of self-gift is only really possible if the Eucharist is not just a *symbol* of Jesus—like a wedding ring, for example—but Jesus himself: his *actual* body, blood, soul, and divinity.

Indeed, Pope Benedict XVI describes the Eucharist as the premier expression of the sacrificial love that Jesus demonstrated on the cross when he writes:

The Eucharist draws us into Jesus' act of self-oblation [self-sacrifice]. More than just statically receiving the incarnate *Logos* ["Word"], we enter into the very dynamic of his self-giving. The imagery of marriage between God and Israel is now realized in a way previously inconceivable: it had meant standing in God's presence, but now it becomes *union with God through sharing in Jesus' self-gift, sharing in his body and blood.* . . . We can thus understand how *agape* [Greek for "sacrificial love"] also became a term for the Eucharist: there God's own *agape* comes to us bodily, in order to continue his work in us and through us. (Benedict XVI, Encyclical Letter, *God Is Love* [*Deus Caritas Est*], nos. 13–14)

For over four hundred years, one of the main debates between Protestants and Catholics has been over whether the Eucharist is a supper that calls to mind the Last Supper of Jesus or a sacrifice that makes present the self-offering of Jesus on Calvary. As Pope Benedict shows, the understanding of the Eucharist as a wedding banquet combines both of these notions into one: the Eucharist is *both a wedding supper and a wedding sacrifice*. It is the "marriage supper of the Lamb" (Revelation 19:9), whose sacrificial love for the Church is expressed by the gift of his body and blood in the Upper Room and on Calvary. In other words, the Eucharist is a "nuptial sacrament" of both the Last Supper and the cross (Benedict XVI, Post-Synodal Apostolic Exhortation Sacrament of Charity [*Sacramentum Caritatis*], no. 27).

MARRIAGE

In our day controversy abounds over the mysterious institution we call "marriage." For some, marriage is a purely human invention, a kind of civil partnership or temporary contract. From this point of view, marriage, like any human institution, is what we make of it. It is not necessarily sacred, or permanent, and it tends to revolve primarily around the personal happiness of the spouses involved, and whether they "love" each other (whatever that may mean). For others, marriage is a divine institution, a sacred covenant rooted in the order of creation and established at the dawn of human history: "Therefore a man leaves his father and his mother and cleaves to his wife, and they become one flesh" (Genesis 2:24). From this point of view, marriage entails the union of the spouses, as well as procreation and the establishment of a family: "Be fruitful and multiply, and fill the earth and subdue it" (Genesis 1:28).

However, when we are confronted with "the great mystery"

of the marriage of Christ and the Church (Ephesians 5:32), we realize that *Christian marriage*—as opposed to other forms of marriage—is more than just a personal contract or a sacred family covenant. Even more, Christian marriage is a *living icon* of the sacrificial spousal love between Christ and the Church. It is (or it is supposed to be) an outward sign of the invisible mystery of Jesus' love for his bride and the bride's love for him.

The "Great Mystery" and Christian Marriage

Nowhere is this reality more powerfully expressed than in the apostle Paul's letter to the Ephesians. Although we have already glanced at excerpts of this text, it is important to look carefully at the entire teaching about how the mystery of Christ's love for the Church is to be lived out in a Christian marriage. In what has become one of the most difficult passages in the New Testament, Paul says this to Christian wives and husbands:

> Be subject to one another out of reverence for Christ. Wives, submit to your husbands, as to the Lord. For the husband is the head of the wife as Christ is the head of the church, his body, and is himself its Savior. As the church submits to Christ, so let wives also submit in everything to their husbands. Husbands, love your wives, as Christ loved the church and gave himself up for her, that he might sanctify her, having cleansed her by the washing of water with the word, that he might present the church to himself in splendor, without spot or wrinkle or any such thing, that she might be holy and without blemish. Even so husbands should love their wives as their own bodies. He who loves his wife loves himself. For no man ever hates his own flesh, but nourishes and cherishes it, as Christ does the church, because we are members of his body. "For this reason a man

shall leave his father and mother and be joined to his wife, and the two shall become one." *This is a great mystery, and I mean in reference to Christ and the church;* however, let each one of you love his wife as himself, and let the wife see that she respects her husband. (Ephesians 5:21–33)

What are we to make of these words? What does Paul mean when he commands wives to "submit" to their husbands? Does this mean that husbands can lord it over their wives and cite biblical justification for doing so? And what does he mean when he commands husbands to "love" their wives like Christ loved the Church? Does he really need to command love? And what does any of this have to do with the "great mystery" of Jesus' love for the Church? How are the two related?

It should go without saying that I do not have the space to address all the issues raised by this important and controversial passage. A whole book could be written just on Ephesians 5 and its implications for the relationship between husbands and wives. For now, I simply want to make several points about the meaning of Paul's words in their original context and how they have been interpreted in ancient Christian tradition and modern-day papal teaching.

First, when Paul speaks about the "submission" (Greek *hypotasso*) of wives to husbands (Ephesians 5:22, 24), *this in no way implies that the wife is inferior to the husband.* This point can be proven easily since Paul uses the exact same Greek word elsewhere to describe Christ's submission or "subjection" to God the Father: "The Son himself will also be submitted (Greek *hypotasso*) to him who subjected all things to him, that God may be all in all" (1 Corinthians 15:28). Evidently, for Paul, the Son's submission to the Father does not take away from his "equality with God" (Philippians 2:6). In the same way, Paul's description of the submission of a wife to her husband does not take away from (the very Jewish) belief that God creates *both* "male and female" in his "image" and "likeness," and, therefore, they possess *equal dignity* (Genesis 1:26–27). In the words of Pope Pius XI:

> *This subjection, however, does not deny or take away the liberty which fully belongs to the woman both in view of her dignity as a human person,* and in view of her most noble office as wife and mother and companion; nor does it bid her obey her husband's every request if not in harmony with right reason or with the dignity due to wife; nor, in fine, does it imply that the wife should be put on a level with those persons who in law are called minors. . . . *For if the man is the head, the woman is the heart, and as he occupies the chief place in ruling, so she may and ought to claim for herself the chief place in love.* (Pope Pius XI, Encyclical On Christian Marriage [*Casti Connubii*], no. 27)

Notice here that already in 1930, the Pope was emphatic that Paul's teaching in Ephesians 5 in no way implies that women are inferior to men; men and women are equal in dignity. In more recent times, Pope John Paul II likewise insists that "the author [of Ephesians] does not intend to say that the husband is the 'master' of the wife and that the interpersonal covenant proper to marriage is a contract of domination by the husband over the wife . . . Husband and wife are, in fact, 'subject to one another' [Ephesians 5:21], mutually subordinated one to another. The source of this reciprocal submission lies in Christian *pietas* [piety] and *its expression is love.*"

Second, with this in mind, it's important to clarify that Paul is *not* saying that the relationship between Christ and the Church is "like" a human marriage. That would be getting him completely backwards. To the contrary, Paul is saying that Christian marriage between a man and a woman should be *like* the supernatural love between Christ and the Church. It is Christ's relationship with the Church that is the "great mystery" (Greek *mysterion mega*) to which Christian marriage must look as its model (Ephesians 5:32). As soon we recognize this point, it goes without saying that any misogynistic or chauvinistic interpretation of Paul's teaching is completely ruled out. For Christ's sacrificial love for the Church is the complete *opposite* of the kind of domination and power struggle that so frequently plagues ordinary relations between men and women. Jesus' self-gift to the Church is *sacrificial "love"* (Greek *agapē*), which he expresses above all by laying down his life on the cross for his bride (Ephesians 5:25). Therefore, Paul is calling the Christian husband to take the role of spiritual leadership through self-sacrificial love, and in this way to act as a kind of "living icon" of Christ the Bridegroom. Likewise, Paul is instructing the Christian wife to place herself "under the mission" (as in the Latin, *sub-missio*) of her husband's sacrificial love, and in this way to act as a living icon of the Church.

Third, and finally, the goal of Christian marriage is not just to emulate the marriage of Christ and the Church. Its purpose is also to bring about *the sanctification and salvation of the spouses*. For many, if not most people, the primary goals of marriage are the companionship of spouses (union) and the procreation of children. For Paul, the deeper aim of Christian marriage is also the eternal salvation of the husband and wife. For Jesus the Bridegroom loved his bride and died for her not just to be united to her and to produce spiritual children of God, but also so "that she might be holy and without blemish" (Ephesians 5:27)—in other words, so that she might be saved. In the same way, the primary goal of Christian spouses should be one another's sanctification and salvation.

In sum, for Saint Paul, Christian marriage is not just modeled on Christ's love for the Church. Like Baptism and the Eucharist, marriage is a mystical *participation* in the spousal and sacrificial relationship between Christ and the Church, in which he lays down his life to be united to her and to save her, and she gives herself back to him as a spouse in response to his love.

The "High Standard" of Spousal Love

Among the Church Fathers, arguably no one grasped Saint Paul's insight into the mystery of marriage more completely than did Saint John Chrysostom. In his homilies on Ephesians, John Chrysostom left us with what are arguably some of the most beautiful and challenging words ever penned on Christian marriage when he says to husbands:

> *Pay attention to love's high standard.* If you take the premise that your wife should submit to you as the church submits to Christ, then you should also take the same kind of careful, sacrificial thought for her that Christ takes for the Church. *Even if you must offer your own life for her, you must not refuse. Even if you must undergo countless struggles on her behalf and have all kinds of things to endure and suffer, you must not refuse. Even if you suffer all this, you have still not done as much as Christ has for the church. For you are already married when you act this way, whereas Christ is acting for one who has rejected and hated him.* So just as he, when she was rejecting, hating, spurning and nagging him, brought her to trust him by his great solicitude, not by threatening, lording it over her or intimidating her or anything like that, so you must also act toward your wife. Even if you see her looking down on you, nagging and despising you, you will be able to win her over with your great love and affection for her. (John Chrysostom, *Homily on Ephesians,* 20:5:25)

What a vision of marital love! And from well over a thousand years ago! Following the lead of Paul, John Chrysostom commands the Christian husband to strive to be a living icon of Jesus the Bridegroom. He makes the important point that in the final analysis, no human love could ever compare to the love of Christ; Christian marriage remains but an "image" of the perfect love of God. Nevertheless, because marriage is supposed to reflect Christ's love for the Church, there is no excuse for male domination or intimidation. Likewise, when the Christian wife supports her husband and respects him by refusing to criticize him or tear him down, she too becomes a living icon of the Church's joyful response to the sacrificial love of Jesus the Bridegroom.

For John Chrysostom, as for Saint Paul, the ultimate goal of Christian marriage is the sanctification and salvation of the spouses. Speaking once again to husbands, Chrysostom writes beautifully:

> Tell her that you love her more than your own life, because this present life is nothing, and that your only hope is that the two of you pass through this life in such a way that in the world to come you will be united in perfect love. Say to her, *"Our time here is brief and fleeting, but if we are pleasing to God, we can exchange this life for the Kingdom to come. Then we will be perfectly one both with Christ and each other, and our pleasure will know no bounds."*
> (John Chrysostom, *Homily on Ephesians,* 20)

Notice that for John Chrysostom, although Christian marriage will pass away in the resurrection, that does not mean that spouses will no longer be united to each other. To the contrary, spouses will be infinitely closer when the earthly sign of marriage gives way to the eternal reality of perfect union with God and one another.

Marriage as a Participation in the Cross

Significantly, one does not have to go back a thousand years to find such insights into the mystery of marriage. In more recent times Popes Leo XIII, Pius XI, Pius XII, and John Paul II, just to a name a few modern Church leaders, have all written extensively on marriage in general and on the words of Saint Paul in the letter to the Ephesians in particular. Given our focus on the relationship between Christian marriage and the mystery of Jesus' spousal love for the Church, I would like to highlight just two aspects of these teachings.

First, in its teaching on matrimony, the *Catechism of the Catholic Church* says that marriage is not just a visible sign of Christ's love for the Church. Even more, Christian marriage bestows on the husband and wife a supernatural power that flows directly from the crucifixion:

> It is by following Christ, renouncing themselves, and taking up their crosses that spouses will be able to "receive" the original meaning of marriage and live it with the help of Christ. *This grace of Christian marriage is a fruit of Christ's cross, the source of all life.* This is what the Apostle makes clear when he says, "Husbands, love your wives, as Christ loved the church and gave himself up for her, that he might sanctify her" [Ephesians 5:25–26]. (CCC 1615–1616)

In other words, it is the cross of Jesus the Bridegroom that gives marriage the power to be an image of the love between him and the Church. Contrary to the popular dictum, Christian marriage is not a "ball and chain"; it is a *cross*. In other words, by its very nature, Christian marriage involves the spouses willingly sharing in each other's sufferings, out of love. Both husband and wife are called to lay down their lives for one another, in good times and in bad, in sickness and in health, for richer or for poorer, for as long as they both shall live.

Seen through this lens, it is small wonder that Jesus of Nazareth and his disciples, from ancient times to today, have stood virtually alone in declaring Christian marriage to be indissoluble (see Matthew 5:31–32; Mark 10:11–12; Luke 16:18; 1 Corinthians 7:10–11). For the bond between Christ the Bridegroom and the Church is one that, unlike countless earthly marriages, will never be broken—not even by death. It is this Jesus—Jesus the Bridegroom—who says in the Gospel: "What therefore God has joined together, let no man put asunder" (Matthew 19:6). The love of Christ is not "till further notice."

An Earthly Foretaste of the Wedding of the Lamb

Second, as the *Catechism* goes on to say, Christian marriage is nothing less than a supernatural mystery, through which husband and wife both participate in the passion and death of Jesus and anticipate the glory of the eternal marriage in heaven:

> "[O]ur Savior, the spouse of the Church, now encounters Christian spouses through the sacrament of Matrimony." Christ dwells with them, gives them the strength to take up their crosses and so follow him, to rise again after they have fallen, to forgive one another, to bear one another's burdens, to "be subject to one another out of reverence for Christ" [Ephesians 5:21], and to love one another with supernatural, tender, and fruitful love. *In the joys of their love and family life he gives them here on earth a foretaste of the wedding feast of the Lamb.* (CCC 1642)

This is the key to understanding the sacraments as nuptial mysteries: baptism, the Eucharist, and Christian marriage are all *participations* in the mystery of the passion, death, and resurrection of the Bridegroom—which, as this entire book has tried to show—are nothing less than mysteries of divine love.

VIRGINITY

Before bringing this chapter to a close, there is one last aspect of the Christian life that it would be remiss of me not to include in our study of Christ the Bridegroom: the mystery of Christian virginity, also referred to as "consecrated celibacy." (Although they have slightly different connotations, in what follows, I will use the two terms interchangeably to refer to the state of voluntary renunciation of married life and consecration of oneself to God.)

For many today, voluntary celibacy is considered a bizarre, "unnatural," and all but inexplicable practice. Although Jesus lived a celibate life, for some reason the idea of anyone else renouncing marriage is frequently looked upon with suspicion, even by many Christians. For others, the celibate life could be seen primarily as an easy way of avoiding the difficulties of marriage. Think here of how the disciples react to Jesus' prohibition of divorce and remarriage: "If that is the case of a man with his wife," they say, "it is better not to marry" (Matthew 19:12 NAB). For still others, celibacy and virginity are primarily a way of devoting oneself entirely to the work of God, without the distractions and duties of family life. As the apostle Paul teaches:

> The unmarried man (Greek *agamos*) is anxious about the affairs of the Lord, how to please the Lord; but the married man is anxious about worldly affairs, how to please his wife, and his

interests are divided. And the unmarried woman or girl (Greek
parthenos) is anxious about the affairs of the Lord, how to be
holy in body and spirit; but the married woman is anxious
about worldly affairs, how to please her husband. (1 Corinthians 7:32–34)

When we look at the mystery of virginity and celibacy in light
of all that we've learned about Jesus the Bridegroom, the voluntary renunciation of earthly marriage takes on an eschatological
meaning. In other words, this state of life points our gaze forward
to the "end" of time (Greek *eschaton*). For if, as Jesus teaches, there
will be no marriage in the resurrection (Mark 12:18–27), then
those who do not marry but rather consecrate themselves to God
become *living signs of the celibate life that everyone will live at the end
of time,* when all of redeemed humanity will be united to God in
the virginal union of Christ and the Church.

Virginity for the Sake of the Kingdom of Heaven

Although Jesus nowhere connects voluntary celibacy with his
identity as the Bridegroom Messiah, he does connect the renunciation of marriage to the future kingdom of heaven. After
the disciples respond to his prohibition of remarriage by declaring that "it is better not to marry," Jesus utters this mysterious
declaration:

> "Not all men can receive this precept, but only those to whom
> it is given. For there are eunuchs who have been so from birth,
> and there are eunuchs who have been made eunuchs by men,
> and *there are eunuchs who have made themselves eunuchs for the sake
> of the kingdom of heaven.* He who is able to receive this, let him
> receive it." (Matthew 19:11–12)

Although much could be said about this passage, for now let it suffice to say that Jesus is using the image of a eunuch—a man incapable of procreation—to describe three categories of people: (1) those who are childless because they are born incapable of procreation; (2) those who are childless because they have been sterilized by others; and (3) those who give up marriage and children for the sake of the kingdom of heaven.

It is the last condition, "eunuchs for the sake of the kingdom of heaven," which is most important for us. By connecting voluntary celibacy to the coming kingdom of God, Jesus reveals that this state of life is an eschatological sign of future glory. In the words of New Testament scholar Lucian Legrand:

> Like the miracles and the sacraments, virginity is a "sign of the Kingdom," an anticipated realization of the final transformation, the glory of the world to come breaking in on the present condition. Such is the sense of [Matthew] 19:12. Jesus and many of those who follow him refrain from sexual activity "in view of the Kingdom," that is, to live already now the life of the world to come.... As with their preaching and their miracles, Jesus and his disciples by their virginity proclaim the advent of the Kingdom. *They exemplify in this world the future condition of men in the next aeon.*

Virginity and the Future Glory of the Resurrection

This eschatological meaning is precisely what many Church Fathers emphasized when they explained the nature of Christian virginity.

For example, in his comments on Jesus' teaching that there will be no marriage in the resurrection, Saint Cyprian, the third-century bishop of Carthage, declares:

Virgins, persevere in what you have begun to be. Persevere in what you will be. A great reward, a glorious prize for virtue, and an excellent reward for purity are reserved for you. . . . The voice of the Lord says, "Those who will be found worthy of that world and of the resurrection from the dead, they neither marry nor are given in marriage . . ." (Luke 20:35). *What we shall be, you have already begun to be. You already have in this world the glory of the resurrection.* (Cyprian of Carthage, *The Dress of Virgins,* 22)

Along similar lines, Saint Ambrose describes consecrated virgins as "brides of God," for whom the glorious wedding of God and his people in the resurrection is already a present reality:

She is a virgin who is *the bride of God,* a harlot who makes gods for herself. What shall I say of the resurrection of which you already hold the rewards? "For in the resurrection they will neither be given in marriage nor marry. . . ." *That which is promised to us is already present with you,* and the object of your prayers is with you; you are of this world, and yet not in this world. This age has held you, but has not been able to retain you. (Ambrose, *Concerning Virgins* 1.9.52)

For the early Church Fathers, the voluntary renunciation of marriage was far from bizarre, or unnatural, much less unbiblical. It was a sign in this life on earth of the future reality, in which there will be no marriage in the resurrection, because all of God's people will be wedded to Christ in the Church.

Virginity, Celibacy, and Christ the Bridegroom Today

In our day and time, this connection between the mysteries of consecrated virginity and celibacy and Jesus' identity as Bridegroom has been elaborated with amazing profundity and beauty. For our purposes here, I will conclude by highlighting three key emphases of contemporary Church teaching. And here I wish to follow the Church in making a distinction between the celibacy of priests and the consecration of women to a life of virginity.

On one hand, women who consecrate themselves to God as virgins and renounce marriage for the religious life are nothing less than *brides of God,* spouses of Christ. Consider, for example, the beautiful words from the contemporary Catholic rite of consecration to a life of virginity, spoken by the bishop:

> [Lord,] among your many gifts you give to some the grace of virginity. Yet the honor of marriage is in no way lessened. As it was in the beginning, your first blessing still remains upon this holy union. *Yet your loving wisdom chooses those who make sacrifice of marriage for the sake of the love of which it is the sign. They renounce the joys of human marriage, but cherish all that it foreshadows. (Rite of Consecration to a Life of Virginity,* Prayer of Consecration, no. 24)

As the words of this rite reveal, the entire life of each consecrated woman speaks to this world about the reality of the world to come, in which there is no earthly marriage, but rather the fulfillment of the unbreakable covenant with Christ, "the Bridegroom of Virgins." Note well that this eschatological vision of consecrated virginity in no way takes away from the goodness of matrimony, but instead reinforces it by pointing us to the perfect love that marriage foreshadows.

On the other hand, men who consecrate themselves to God in a life of celibacy as priests take on a somewhat different role. By means of their priestly celibacy, they become icons of Christ the Bridegroom in his love for the Church. In the words of Pope John Paul II:

The priest is called to be the living image of Jesus Christ, the spouse of the Church. Of course, he will always remain a member of the community as a believer alongside his other brothers and sisters . . . , but in virtue of his configuration to Christ, the head and shepherd, the priest stands in this spousal relationship with regard to the community. . . . In his spiritual life, therefore, he is called to live out Christ's spousal love toward the Church, his bride. (John Paul II, Post-Synodal Apostolic Exhortation on the Formation of Priests in the Circumstances of the Present Day [*Pastores Dabo Vobis*], no. 22)

In other words, the priest is called to make a complete gift of himself, body and soul, to the Church, the bride of Christ, similar to the way that a husband gives of himself for his wife. Indeed, in some ways, the priest's gift of himself to the Church is even *more* like Christ's gift of himself to his bride, because it is virginal, supernatural, and fulfilled above all in the sacrificial wedding banquet of the Eucharist.

Finally, all forms of Christian renunciation of marriage are ultimately rooted in the reality of Jesus' identity as Bridegroom and the hope for the eternal wedding of Christ and the Church. In the beautiful words of the *Catechism of the Catholic Church:*

Christ is the center of all Christian life. The bond with him takes precedence over all other bonds, familial or social. From the very beginning of the Church there have been men and women who have renounced the great good of marriage to follow the Lamb wherever he goes, to be intent on the things of the Lord, to seek to please him, *and to go out to meet the Bridegroom who is coming.* . . . *Virginity for the sake of the kingdom of heaven* is an unfolding of baptismal grace, *a powerful sign of the supremacy of the bond with Christ and of the ardent expectation of his return, a sign which also recalls that marriage is a reality of this present age which is passing away.* Both the sacrament of Matrimony and virginity for the Kingdom of God come from the Lord himself. It is he who gives them meaning and grants them the grace which is indispensable for living them out in conformity with his will. Esteem of virginity for the sake of the kingdom and the Christian understanding of marriage are inseparable, and they reinforce each other. (CCC 1618–1620)

In short, according to the New Testament, ancient Christian tradition, and contemporary Church teaching, every single Christian, whether single or married, man or woman, priest or virgin, monk or nun, husband or wife—every single baptized person—is inextricably caught up in the "great mystery" of the love of God for his people. This love, shown in so many ways, above all has been poured out in the life, death, resurrection, and return of Jesus, the divine Bridegroom Messiah. If we have the eyes to see it—that is, if we can learn to see Jesus through ancient Jewish eyes—then the entire Christian life does indeed bear the marks of the spousal love of Christ for each and every one of us.

7

Beside the Well with Jesus

In bringing this book to a close, I'd like to go back for a moment to the story of Jesus and the woman at the well (John 4:1–42). As we have already seen, the Samaritan woman was not what some would call "marriage material"—at least, not for any ordinary bridegroom. She was a woman with a past, with all the baggage and wounds and shame that go with sin. She wasn't from a great race of people, or the elite sectors of society, and her religious ideas were a mix of truth and error. She apparently wasn't well accepted by her own people, and she had to carry out the daily task of drawing water alone.

Yet Jesus was waiting for her at the well. He, the divine Bridegroom come in person, he through whom the world was made, sat there, waiting to ask *her* for a drink and wanting her to ask *him* for a gift: the gift of the "living water" that would cleanse her from sins, quench her deepest thirst, and unite her to him as her Messiah.

As soon as we see Jesus this way, we realize: *the Samaritan woman is every one of us.* She is every human being who has ever sinned and betrayed the God who loved us and made us, by chasing after other gods, trying desperately to get creatures to give us what only the Creator can give. She is every human being who has ever made a complete mess of their lives with choices from which they just can't seem to break loose. She is every human person who has a sinful and broken past that they'd just rather not talk about.

But none of this stops Jesus from pursuing her. Nor does it stop him from pursuing us. After all these centuries, he is *still waiting* at the well. He is waiting for us to ask him for the gift of living water, and, even more, for the gift of himself. In order to receive the gift, however, like the Samaritan woman, we've got to come clean about our past. We have to own up to our sin, to be truthful about who we are, and tell him how many gods we've chased. It's no use pulling her evasive maneuver and trying to switch the subject; he already knows "everything we've ever done" (cf. John 4:29). And he is waiting by the well *anyway*. In the beautiful words of the *Catechism of the Catholic Church:*

> "If you knew the gift of God!" [John 4:10]. The wonder of prayer is revealed beside the well where we come seeking water: *there, Christ comes to meet every human being. It is he who first seeks us and asks us for a drink. Jesus thirsts; his asking arises from the depths of God's desire for us.* Whether we realize it or not, prayer is the encounter of God's thirst with ours. *God thirsts that we may thirst for him.* (CCC 2560)

That is the last mystery of the Christian life that is lit up by the reality of Jesus the Bridegroom: the mystery of prayer. It is not only in baptism and the Eucharist, or through marriage, consecrated virginity, or priestly celibacy that we can enter into the great mystery of Christ's love for the Church. It is also through the *personal encounter* with the living God known as prayer. Jesus not only wants to wash his bride, and to feed her, and to be with her when the marriage supper of the Lamb finally comes; he also wants to talk to her, alone, away from the crowd, at the well of living water.

For if Jesus really is the divine Bridegroom and the Church really is his bride, then he is *always* there, waiting beside the well from all eternity, waiting for us to bring him our brokenness and ask him to give us the gift of his Spirit. And if we do this every day, until the very end of our lives, he will bring us to the land that is called "Married" (*Beulah*) (Isaiah 62:4), where the dead will be raised, and there will be no more "marrying or giving in marriage" (cf. Mark 12:25), for the "marriage of the Lamb" will have finally come and the Bride will have "made herself ready" (Revelation 19:7). On that day, the new Jerusalem will descend from heaven in all her glory, as "a bride adorned for her husband" (Revelation 21:2). Then, when the old world passes away, and a new one comes, in which there is no more crying or pain anymore, because all things have been made new, then we shall finally see the One who loved us and gave himself for us. Then we shall behold him with whom we have sat and talked beside the well, no longer through a mirror dimly, but as he is, "face to face" (1 Corinthians 13:12). And on that day, perhaps we shall even hear the angels sing what was once said to John: "Come, let us show you the Bride, the wife of the Lamb" (Revelation 22:9).

APPENDIX

Jewish Sources Outside the Bible

In order to situate the words and deeds of Jesus in their historical context, we need to be familiar with two key sources of information: (1) the Jewish Scriptures, commonly referred to by Christians as "the Old Testament," and (2) ancient Jewish tradition, enshrined in a whole host of writings not contained in the Hebrew Bible and often not readily accessible to non-Jewish readers who are not already specialists in biblical studies.

For this reason, it is helpful to briefly identify the various collections of Jewish writings outside the Bible that I refer to over the course of this book. (The reader may want to mark this page for reference.) I cannot overemphasize here that I am not suggesting that Jesus himself (or even the writers of the New Testament) would have *read* any of these works, some of which were compiled long after he lived and died. What I am suggesting is that many of these writings bear witness to ancient Jewish *traditions* outside the Bible that may have circulated at the time of Jesus. In particular, there are Jewish phrases, customs, practices, and beliefs reflected in both the New Testament and these extrabiblical Jewish writings, traditions that appear to be taken for granted by Jesus and the first Jewish Christians and which sometimes demand explanation because they are not referred to in Jewish Scripture (such as the expression "friend of the bridegroom" in John 3:29 or "sons of the bridechamber" in Mark 2:19).

In light of this situation, contemporary scholars such as Dale Allison, Maurice Casey, Craig Keener, John Meier, James Dunn, Craig Evans, Geza Vermes, and many others make abundant use of extrabiblical Jewish sources in their study of the words and deeds of Jesus. Indeed, the burgeoning scholarly interest in the Jewish context of Christianity is on full display in *The Jewish Annotated New Testament* (eds. Amy-Jill Levine and Marc Zvi Brettler, Oxford University Press, 2011), in which an international team of Jewish scholars utilizes both Jewish Scripture and extrabiblical writings, including rabbinic literature, to shed light on the meaning of the New Testament.

With this in mind, after the writings in the Bible itself, the most important Jewish sources utilized by contemporary scholars are the following:

- *The Dead Sea Scrolls:* an ancient collection of Jewish manuscripts copied sometime between the second century B.C. and A.D. 70. This collection contains numerous writings from the Second Temple period, during which Jesus lived.
- *The Pseudepigrapha:* a vast array of writings that are often attributed to ancient authors such as Enoch, Ezra, Baruch, and others, and that span the centuries before and after the time of Jesus (the second century B.C. through the fourth century A.D.). Many of these works, such as 1 Enoch, Jubilees, 4 Ezra, 2 Baruch, give key insights into Judaism during the Second Temple period.

- *The Works of Josephus:* Josephus was a Jewish historian and Pharisee who lived in the first century A.D. His works are extremely important witnesses to Jewish history and culture at the time of Jesus and the early Church.
- *The Mishnah* and *Tosefta:* These are two extensive collections of the oral traditions of Jewish rabbis who lived from about 50 B.C. to A.D. 200. Most of the traditions are focused on legal and liturgical matters. For rabbinic Judaism, outside the Bible, the Mishnah remains the most authoritative witness to Jewish tradition.
- *The Targums:* These are ancient Jewish translations and paraphrases of parts of the Jewish Scriptures from Hebrew into Aramaic. These texts emerged sometime after the Babylonian exile (587 B.C.), when many Jews began speaking Aramaic instead of Hebrew. Scholars disagree about their exact dates.
- *The Babylonian Talmud:* This is a vast compilation—more than thirty massive volumes—of the traditions of Jewish rabbis who lived from around A.D. 220 to A.D. 500. The Talmud consists of both legal opinions and biblical interpretation, in the form of an extensive commentary on the Mishnah.
- *The Midrashim:* These texts are ancient Jewish commentary on various books of the Bible. Although parts of these are later than the Talmud, they contain many interpretations of Scripture attributed to rabbis who lived during the times of the Mishnah and Talmud.

These are by no means all of the ancient Jewish writings that are relevant for understanding the New Testament, but they are the ones I will engage from time to time in this book.

NOTES

Introduction

4   **"the sons of the bridechamber"**: author's translation.

    "The Son of God, by becoming incarnate": Unless otherwise noted, all translations of the Catechism cited herein are taken from the *Catechism of the Catholic Church* (2d ed.; Vatican City: Libreria Editrice Vaticana, 1997).

1. The Divine Love Story

7   **"*What God* don't you believe in?"**: Cf. N. T. Wright, *The New Testament and the People of God* (Minneapolis: Fortress, 1992), xiv–xv; Tom Wright, *The Original Jesus: The Life and Vision of a Revolutionary* (Grand Rapids, Mich.: Eerdmans, 1996), 76–87.

12   **"I passed by you again"**: Because of the abundant English archaisms present in the RSV translation of Ezekiel 16:8, for this passage I have used the NRSV.

    "speaks to her heart": Raymond C. Ortlund, *God's Unfaithful Wife: A Biblical Theology of Spiritual Adultery,* New Studies in Biblical Theology 2 (Downers Grove, Ill.: InterVarsity Press, 1996), 68n64. Cf. Genesis 34:3; Judges 19:3; Isaiah 40:2.

"steadfast love": John Bright, *Jeremiah* (Anchor Bible 21; New York: Doubleday, 1965), 14.

13 ***"The Lord came from Sinai"**: Mekilta de Rabbi-Ishmael,* trans. Jacob Z. Lauterbach, 3 vols. (Philadelphia: Jewish Publication Society of America, 1933), 2:218–19.

14 **Such aspects of the pagan cults:** See esp. Ortlund, *God's Unfaithful Wife,* 83; following N. Stienstra, *YHWH Is the Husband of His People: Analysis of a Biblical Metaphor with Special Reference to Translation* (Kampen, The Netherlands: Kok Pharos, 1993), 163: "The actual situation, involving cultic prostitution, interacts with the metaphorical concept. The fact that idolatrous practices actually consisted of sexual acts made the marriage metaphor all the more appropriate for telling the people how badly they behaved with respect to YHWH." Along similar lines, John Oswalt points out: "The heavily sexual orientation of the Canaanite religion meant that ritual prostitution was a fundamental part of worship. Thus it is not merely imagery when it is said [in Isaiah 57:7–8] that those who went to the high places to offer their sacrifices *placed their bed* there." John H. Oswalt, *The Book of Isaiah,* New International Commentary on the Old Testament, 2 vols. (Grand Rapids, Mich.: Eerdmans, 1986, 1998), 2:478, citing W. F. Albright, "The High Place in Ancient Palestine," in International Organization for the Study of the Old Testament, *Volume du Congrès: Strasbourg, 1956,* Vetus Testamentum Supplements 4 (Leiden: Brill, 1957), 242–58. For skepticism in this regard, see Kare van der Toorn, "Prostitution (Cultic)," in *Anchor Bible Dictionary,* ed. David Noel Freedman, 6 vols. (New York: Doubleday, 1992), 5:505–513.

The sin of idolatry is: See G. K. Beale, *We Become What We Worship: A Biblical Theology of Idolatry* (Downers Grove, Ill.: InterVarsity Press, 2008).

17 **a spiritual marriage between God and Israel:** See Michael L. Satlow, *Jewish Marriage in Antiquity* (Princeton, NJ: Princeton University Press, 2001), 54, who notes that this imagery of God's broken marriage with Israel continued in later Jewish tradition, which contains several parables in which "Israel marries, is unfaithful, and then is brought back into covenantal relationship with God."

between God and his faithless bride: For a full study, see Ortlund, *God's Unfaithful Wife,* 25–136.

19 bridal gifts of "steadfast love": J. Andrew Dearman, *The Book of Hosea,* New International Commentary on the New Testament (Grand Rapids, Mich.: Eerdmans, 2010), 127–28.

he will forgive all that she has done: See Francis I. Anderson and David Noel Freedman, *Hosea: A New Translation,* Anchor Bible 24 (New York: Doubleday, 1980), 215.

The God of Israel is not a distant deity: Dearman, *The Book of Hosea,* 128–29.

20 "For thy Maker is thy husband": Unless otherwise noted, all English translations of the Midrash Rabbah [Great Commentary] of the ancient rabbis are taken from *Midrash Rabbah,* trans. and ed. H. Freedman and Maurice Simon, 10 vols. (London/New York: Soncino, 1983).

many different ways to interpret the Song of Songs: For helpful overviews of the history of interpretation, see Roland E. Murphy, *The Song of Songs,* Hermeneia: A Critical and Historical Commentary on the Bible (Minneapolis: Fortress, 1990), 11–41; and Blaise Arminjon, *The Cantata of Love: A Verse by Verse Reading of the Song of Songs* (San Francisco: Ignatius, 1988).

already in the first century: Philip S. Alexander, *The Targum of Canticles,* Aramaic Bible 17a (Collegeville, Minn.: Liturgical Press, 2003), 35: "The Rabbis did not invent the allegorical interpretation: it was probably already rather old in Aqiba's time."

21 "He who sings the Song of Songs": Cf. Babylonian Talmud, *Sanhedrin,* 101a.

There is no competing view: Alexander, *The Targum of Canticles,* 27.

23 Old Testament scholar Ellen Davis: Ellen F. Davis, *Proverbs, Ecclesiastes, and the Song of Songs,* Westminster Bible Companion (Louisville: Westminster John Knox, 2000), 231.

"The Song of Songs is, in a sense": Davis, *Proverbs, Ecclesiastes, and the Song of Songs,* 231.

"at one level of the poet's meaning": Davis, *Proverbs, Ecclesiastes, and the Song of Songs,* 255.

25 encompasses all twelve tribes: See Davis, *Proverbs, Ecclesiastes, and the Song of Songs,* 284–85.

26 "The image of the bride": Davis, *Proverbs, Ecclesiastes, and the Song of Songs,* 269.

the poem never actually describes: "If the 'marriage' in the Song is ever physically consummated, we are told that only indirectly" (Davis, *Proverbs, Ecclesiastes, the Song of Songs*, 252).

27 the bride (Israel) waiting for the bridegroom (God): Davis, *Proverbs, Ecclesiastes, and the Song of Songs*, 3012.
"At the time of our distress": Alexander, *The Targum of Canticles*, 205.

2. Jesus the Bridegroom

29 "I am not the Messiah, but": RSVCE (slightly adapted). I have translated the Greek word *christos* literally as "Messiah," so as to avoid the popular misunderstanding of "Christ" as a personal name.

30 John answered: "You yourselves": author's translation.
he embraced a life of celibacy: See especially John P. Meier, *A Marginal Jew: Rethinking the Historical Jesus*, Anchor (Yale) Bible Reference Library, 5 vols. (New York: Doubleday/New Haven: Yale University Press, 1991, 1994, 2001, 2009), 1:332–45; James H. Charlesworth, *Jesus within Judaism*, Anchor Bible Reference Library (New York: Doubleday, 1988), 72; Geza Vermes, *Jesus the Jew* (Philadelphia: Fortress, 1973), 100–101.

31 John is alluding to a famous biblical prophecy: See, e.g., Adela Yarbro Collins and John J. Collins, *King and Messiah as Song of God: Divine, Human, and Angelic Messianic Figures in Biblical and Related Literature* (Grand Rapids, Mich.: Eerdmans, 2008), 44–45; Walter C. Kaiser, *The Messiah in the Old Testament* (Grand Rapids, Mich.: Zondervan, 1995), 191; Joseph Klausner, *The Messianic Idea in Israel: From Its Beginning to the Completion of the Mishnah*, trans. W. F. Stinespring (London: George Allen & Unwin, 1956), 100–102. Although the word "Messiah" is not present in Jeremiah 33, as Joseph Fitzmyer S.J. points out, the passage was interpreted as a reference to the Messiah in Second Temple Judaism (*The One Who Is to Come* [Grand Rapids, Mich.: Eerdmans, 2007], 28–49). See Craig A. Evans, "The Messiah in the Dead Sea Scrolls," in *Israel's Messiah in the Bible and the Dead Sea Scrolls*, ed. Richard S. Hess and M. Daniel Carroll (Grand Rapids, Mich.: Baker, 2003), 85–102 (here 94–95).

32 "Thus says the LORD: In this place": RSVCE, slightly adapted.
the parallels between this prophecy: See Jocelyn McWhirter, *The*

Bridegroom Messiah and the People of God: Marriage in the Fourth Gospel, Society for New Testament Studies Monograph Series 138 (Cambridge, UK: Cambridge University Press, 2006), 56.

Finally, just as Jeremiah talks: Although McWhirter is correct to point out that Jeremiah never explicitly identifies "the bridegroom" in Jeremiah 33:10–11 as the Messiah (*The Bridegroom Messiah and the People of God,* 57), she fails to note that the oracle about the voice of the bridegroom culminates in God's promise to send the messianic heir of David (Jeremiah 33:17–26). Hence, even if John the Baptist was the first to connect the Messiah with the voice of the bridegroom, it needs to be said that this connection was facilitated by the juxtaposition of the two hopes in Jeremiah 33 itself.

33 **recorded in the Mishnah:** Unless otherwise noted, all translations of the Mishnah cited herein are from *The Mishnah,* trans. Herbert Danby (Oxford, UK: Oxford University Press, 1933). For other rabbinic examples of the *shosbin* as friend of the bridegroom, see *Exodus Rabbah* 20:8; 46:1.

it was the friend of the bridegroom: See Craig S. Keener, *The Gospel of John: A Commentary,* 2 vols. (Peabody, Mass.: Hendrickson, 2003), 1:579.

Babylonian Talmud: Unless otherwise noted, all translations of the Babylonian Talmud are from the *Soncino Talmud,* ed. and trans. Isidore Epstein, 35 vols. (London: Soncino, 1935–1952).

34 **John the Baptist must recede from view:** See Raymond E. Brown, S.S., *The Gospel According to John,* 2 vols., Anchor Bible Reference Library 29 and 30 (New York: Doubleday, 1966, 1970), 1:152.

35 **"On the third day there was a wedding":** RSVCE, slightly adapted.

37 **Although Jesus' response certainly:** See Rudolf Schnackenburg, *The Gospel According to St John,* trans. Kevin Smyth et al., 4 vols. (New York: Herder and Herder, 1968, 1979, 1982), 1:327–28; Brown, *The Gospel According to John,* 1:98–99.

"Honor your father": For an extensive list of texts on honoring one's parents in Judaism, see Craig S. Keener, *The Gospel of John,* 1:505n135.

38 **"The term would be intelligible":** Brown, *The Gospel According to John,* 1:108. See also Edward C. Hoskyns, *The Fourth Gospel* (London: Faber & Faber, 1940), 530.

sound much harsher than it is: "Jesus' reply is not quite as rude in the

Semitic original that it reflects as in some English translations. . . ." For
example, the RSV reads: "What have you to do with me?" See Craig
Blomberg, *The Historical Reliability of John's Gospel* (Downers Grove:
InterVarsity Press, 2001), 86.

Jesus is firmly but respectfully declining: Brown, *The Gospel According to John,* 1:99.

39 **"Simply stating the need, as she does":** Keener, *The Gospel of John,*
    2:503.

40 *an allusion to Jewish Scripture:* Should there be any doubt about the
    possibility that Mary's words are in fact an allusion to Isaiah 24–25, it
    is fascinating to note that the very same prophecy is mentioned in an
    ancient rabbinic tradition about the songs sung at Jewish weddings.
    According to the Mishnah, when the Temple and its Jewish leadership
    were destroyed, it even affected the way Jewish weddings were cele-
    brated: "When the Sanhedrin ceased, *singing ceased at the wedding feasts,*
    as it is written, 'No more do they drink wine with singing. . . .'" [Isaiah
    24:9] (Mishnah *Sotah* 9:11; cf. Tosefta, *Sotah* 15:7).
    On this mountain the LORD of hosts: RSVCE, slightly adapted.
    the messianic banquet: See Dennis E. Smith, "Messianic Banquet," in
    Freedman, ed., *Anchor Bible Dictionary,* 4:787–91; J. Priest, "A Note on
    the Messianic Banquet," in *The Messiah: Developments in Earliest Judaism
    and Christianity,* ed. James H. Charlesworth, First Princeton Sympo-
    sium on Judaism and Christian Origins (Minneapolis: Fortress, 1992),
    222–38; Emil Schürer, *The History of the Jewish People in the Age of Jesus
    Christ (175 B.C.–A.D. 135)* (rev. and ed. Geza Vermes et al.; 4 vols.;
    Edinburgh: T. & T. Clark, 1973, 1979, 1986, 1987), 2.534n73.

42 **If we do the math:** Keener, *The Gospel of John,* 1:511; Schnackenburg,
    The Gospel of St John, 1:332 n. 25.
    one of the marks of the future age of salvation: See Keener, *The
    Gospel of John,* 1:494n19; Brown, *The Gospel According to John,* 1:105.

43 **"And it will happen that":** Unless otherwise noted, all translations of
    the Old Testament Pseudepigrapha contained herein are from *The Old
    Testament Pseudepigrapha,* ed. James H. Charlesworth, 2 vols., Anchor
    Bible Reference Library (New York: Doubleday, 1983, 1985). I have
    slightly adapted the unit of measurement here ("liter" for "cor") for the
    sake of clarity.

44 his responsibility to oversee the quality: Keener, *The Gospel of John,*
    1:514.

45 "When the mother of Jesus says": Adeline Fehribach, *The Women
    in the Life of the Bridegroom: A Feminist Historical-Literary Analysis of the
    Female Characters in the Fourth Gospel* (Collegeville, Minn.: Liturgical
    Press, 1998), 29. She is following in part Mark Stibbe, *John* (Sheffield,
    UK: JSOT Press, 1993), 46; and Raymond Collins, "Mary in the Fourth
    Gospel: A Decade of Johannine Studies," *Louvain Studies* 3 (1970):
    125–26.

    "[An ancient reader] would have realized": Fehribach, *The Women
    in the Life of the Bridegroom,* 30; following Sandra Schneiders, *The Re-
    velatory Text: Interpreting the New Testament as Sacred Scripture* (San Fran-
    cisco: Harper, 1991), 187.

46 he uses the expression in a technical way: See Keener, *The Gospel of
    John,* 1:507; André Feuillet, "The Hour of Jesus and the Sign of Cana,"
    in *Johannine Studies,* trans. Thomas E. Crane (Staten Island: Alba House,
    1964), 17–37.

49 *"the [new] covenant":* The word "new" is in brackets because it is miss-
    ing from some manuscripts of the Gospels of Matthew and Mark.
    Nevertheless, as commentators note, even without the exact word, in
    all four accounts Jesus is *de facto* instituting a new covenant, since the old
    covenants were not ratified with the blood of Jesus. See W. D. Davies
    and Dale C. Allison, Jr., *The Gospel According to Saint Matthew,* 3 vols.,
    International Critical Commentary on Scripture (Edinburgh: T. & T.
    Clark, 1988, 1991, 1997), 3:464–65; I. Howard Marshall, *Last Supper
    and Lord's Supper* (Exeter: Paternoster, 1980), 92.

    hearing Jesus refer to the "blood" of the "covenant": See, for ex-
    ample, Kim Huat Tan, *The Zion Traditions and the Aims of Jesus,* Soci-
    ety of New Testament Studies Monograph Series 91 (Cambridge, UK:
    Cambridge University Press, 1997), 206–27, 216; Davies and Allison,
    The Gospel According to Saint Matthew, 3:372–77; Joseph A. Fitzmyer,
    The Gospel According to Luke, 2 vols., Anchor Bible 28–28A (New York:
    Doubleday, 1983, 1985), 2:1391.

50 Jesus' actions at the Last Supper: "The upper room is a 'new Sinai'"
    (John Ronning, *The Jewish Targums and John's Logos Theology* [Grand
    Rapids, Mich.: Baker Academic, 2010], 154).

"You are those who have continued with me": RSVCE, slightly adapted.

51 "In the Last Supper, [Jesus] was": Claude Chavasse, *The Bride of Christ: An Enquiry into the Nuptial Element in Early Christianity* (London: Religious Book Club, 1939), 60–61.

52 now he addresses Mary as "Woman": See Joseph Ratzinger (Pope Benedict XVI), *Jesus of Nazareth: Holy Week: From the Entrance into Jerusalem to the Resurrection,* trans. Vatican Secretariat of State (San Francisco: Ignatius, 2011), 2:221–22.

54 *"Jesus once in Cana of Galilee":* Cited in Joel C. Elowsky, *John,* 2 vols., Ancient Christian Commentary on Scripture, New Testament IVb (Downers Grove, Ill.: InterVarsity Press, 2007), 1:98.

3. The Woman at the Well

56 entire books have been written: See especially Fehribach, *Women in the Life of the Bridegroom;* and McWhirter, *The Bridegroom Messiah and the People of God,* for scholarly studies of these bridal figures in the Gospels.

59 the Samaritan woman looks suspiciously: On the Samaritan woman as a bridal figure evocative of brides in Jewish Scripture, see especially McWhirter, *The Bridegroom Messiah and the People of God,* 58–76; Fehribach, *Women in the Life of the Bridegroom,* 45–58; Francis J. Moloney, *The Gospel of John,* ed. Daniel J. Harrington, Sacra Pagina 4 (Collegeville, Minn.: Liturgical Press, 1998), 121; Calum Carmichael, "Marriage and the Samaritan Woman," *New Testament Studies* 26 (1980): 332–46; Normand R. Bonneau, "The Woman at the Well, John 4, and Genesis 24," *The Bible Today* 67 (1973): 1252–59; Hoskyns, *The Fourth Gospel,* 263.

61 Male Foreigner + Woman: Fehribach, *Women in the Life of the Bridegroom,* 50–51.

62 "the initial elements of a betrothal type-scene": Fehribach, *Women in the Life of the Bridegroom,* 50–51.

the historical origins of the Samaritan people: On the Samaritans, see Robert T. Anderson, "Samaritans," in Freedman, ed., *Anchor Bible Dictionary,* 5:940–47.

64 an extraordinarily unlikely prospect: On divorce and remarriage for

Jewish women, see Tal Ilan, *Jewish Women in Greco-Roman Palestine* (Peabody, Mass.: Hendrickson, 1996), 135–57; Tal Ilan, *Integrating Women into Second Temple History* (Peabody, Mass.: Hendrickson, 1999), 43–63. On divorce and remarriage in Jesus' time, see especially Meier, *A Marginal Jew,* 4:84–94.

"Do not add marriage to marriage": This translation is from Charlesworth, ed., *Old Testament Pseudepigrapha,* 2:581.

In her current situation: For further references to the immorality of premarital and extramarital relations in ancient Judaism, see Keener, *The Gospel of John,* 1:594.

65 *a symbol of the people of Samaria:* See McWhirter, *The Bridegroom Messiah and the People of God,* 69n77; Fehribach, *Women in the Life of the Bridegroom,* 58–69; Hendrikus Boers, *Neither on This Mountain Nor in Jerusalem: A Study of John 4,* Society of Biblical Literature 35 (Atlanta: Scholars Press, 1988); C. K. Barrett, *The Gospel According to St. John,* 2d ed. (Philadelphia: Westminster, 1978), 235; C. H. Dodd, *The Interpretation of the Fourth Gospel* (Cambridge, UK: Cambridge University Press, 1953), 313–14.

66 **prophetic signs were supposed to set**: See Scot McKnight, "Jesus and Prophetic Actions," *Bulletin for Biblical Research* 10 (2000): 197–232; Meier, *A Marginal Jew,* 3:153; N. T. Wright, *Jesus and the Victory of God,* Christian Origins and the Question of God, vol. 2 (Minneapolis: Fortress, 1996), 558.

67 **two of the seven deities**: "The first-century reader would have perceived Jesus' reference to the five husbands as a symbolic reference to the foreign gods of the five groups of people brought in by the Assyrians to colonize Samaria (cf. 2 Kgs 17:13–34). Although some scholars reject this notion, the basic objection to the five husbands symbolizing the former gods of those who colonized Samaria is that 2 Kgs 17:13–34 actually refers to seven gods, with two groups having two gods. This problem, however, could be resolved if one accepted Gerard Sloyan's interpretation of 2 Kgs 17:13–34. Sloyan implies that two of the seven deities are consorts. This would make the number of male gods to be five, and only the male gods of the Samaritan people would have been symbolized by the woman's five former husbands" (Fehribach, *Women in the Life of the Bridegroom,* 65–66). Here Fehribach is citing Gerard Sloyan, "The Samaritans in the New Testament," *Horizons* 10 (1983): 10.

Josephus emphasizes the number five: Josephus writes: "But now the Cutheans, who removed into Samaria, (for that is the name they have been called by to this time, because they were brought out of the country called Cuthah, which is a country of Persia, and there is a river of the same name in it,) each of them, according to their nations, which were in number five, brought their own gods into Samaria" (Josephus, *Antiquities* 9.14.3).

"Jesus' statement to the woman": Fehribach, *Women in the Life of the Bridegroom,* 67. So too McWhirter, *The Bridegroom Messiah and the People of God,* 71–72.

68   **he is initiating the time:** "[I]f the scene itself is symbolically the incorporation of Samaria into the New Israel, the bride of the new Bridegroom . . . , then the adultery/idolatry symbolism so prevalent in the prophetic literature for speaking of Israel's infidelity to Yahweh the Bridegroom would be a most apt vehicle for discussion of the anomalous religious situation of Samaria" (Schneiders, *The Revelatory Text,* 190). Cited in Fehribach, *Women in the Life of the Bridegroom,* 67.

70   **a bridegroom would make his intentions known:** See John J. Collins, "Marriage, Divorce, and Family in Second Temple Judaism," in *Families in Ancient Israel,* ed. Leo G. Perdue et al. (Louisville: Westminster John Knox, 1997), 113–15; Roland de Vaux, *Ancient Israel: Its Life and Institutions,* trans. John McHugh (repr., Grand Rapids, Mich.: Eerdmans, 1998), 26–28; John L. Comaroff, ed., *The Meaning of Marriage Payments* (New York: Academic Press, 1980).

the expression "living water": Keener, *The Gospel of John,* 1:604; cf. Genesis 26:19; Leviticus 14:5–6.

71   **"And when Jacob saw Rachel":** *Targum Pseudo-Jonathan: Genesis,* trans. Michael Maher MSC (Collegeville, Minn.: Liturgical Press, 1992). Another version reads: "When Jacob had gone, the shepherds stood by the well but found no water. And they waited three days (to see) if perhaps it might flow. But it did not flow. Therefore Laban was told on the third day, and he knew that Jacob had fled, *because it was through his merits that it had flowed for twenty years*" (*Targum Pseudo-Jonathan* on Genesis 31:22).

72   **the *ritual water* used in the Tabernacle of Moses:** See Baruch A. Levine, *Numbers 1–20,* Anchor Bible 4A (New York: Doubleday, 1993), 468.

73 **Jewish pilgrims could be cleansed:** For two excellent studies of Jewish ritual washing, see Jonathan D. Lawrence, *Washing in Water: Trajectories of Ritual Bathing in the Hebrew Bible and Second Temple Literature* (Atlanta: Society of Biblical Literature, 2006); Jonathan D. Lawrence, "Washing, Ritual," in *The Eerdmans Dictionary of Early Judaism*, ed. John J. Collins and Daniel C. Harlow (Grand Rapids, Mich.: Eerdmans, 2010), 1331–32.

    the custom of a Jewish bride: On the bridal bath in ancient Israel, see Daniel Bodi, "Ezekiel," in *Zondervan Illustrated Biblical Backgrounds Commentary*, Vol. 4, *Isaiah, Jeremiah, Lamentations, Ezekiel Daniel*, ed. John H. Walton (Grand Rapids, Mich.: Zondervan, 2009), 438; Block, *The Book of Ezekiel*, 2 vols., New International Commentary on the Old Testament (Grand Rapids, Mich.: Eerdmans, 1997, 1998), 1:484, citing S. Greengus, "Old Babylonian Marriage Ceremonies and Rites," *Journal of Cuneiform Studies* 20 (1966): 57, 61, regarding Ur Excavation Texts 5 636, which mentions a "day of bathing" as a part of the Ancient Near Eastern marriage ritual. In later Jewish tradition, see Michael Kaufman, *Love, Marriage, and Family in Jewish Law and Tradition* (London: Jason Aronson, 1996), 164–65.

75 **"Wash her, anoint her, have her outfitted":** Translation by Judah Goldin, *The Fathers According to Rabbi Nathan* (New Haven, Conn.: Yale University Press, 1955), 172.

76 **the waters flowing from the heart of Jesus:** See Schnackenburg, *The Gospel According to St. John*, 2:152–57; Ratzinger (Benedict XVI), *Jesus of Nazareth: From the Baptism in the Jordan to the Transfiguration*, trans. Adrian J. Walker (New York: Doubleday, 2007), 1:245–46.

77 **a river of living water that will flow:** See Dale C. Allison Jr., "The Living Water (John 4:10–14; 6:35c; 7:37–39)," *St. Vladimir's Theological Quarterly* 30 (1986): 143–57.

78 **a new temple, new worship, and a river of living water:** On the Jewish hope for a new Temple, see T. Desmond Alexander and Simon Gathercole, *Heaven on Earth: The Temple in Biblical Theology* (Carlisle: Paternoster, 2004); R. J. McKelvey, *The New Temple: The Church in the New Testament* (London: Oxford University Press, 1969), 9–24.

79 **Jesus gives up both his "spirit":** In making this connection, it is important not to pit water and spirit against one another. It is not either water or spirit that Jesus gives; it is both. In ancient Jewish thought,

"water" and "spirit" have been connected with one another since the dawn of creation, when the "Spirit" of God hovered "over the face of the waters" like a bird (Genesis 1:1–2). See Joseph Ratzinger (Pope Benedict XVI), *Jesus of Nazareth*, 1:238–48, for an excellent discussion of the connections between the living water and the Spirit.

80 **"It is pertinent to the image of the reality":** Cited in Elowsky, *John*, 2:146–47.

81 **the words of Saint Methodius, the ancient Christian bishop:** Cited in Elowsky, *John*, 2:156–57.

4. The Crucifixion

84 **The Sons of the Bridechamber:** In what follows, I will be translating the expression "sons of the bridechamber" literally (Mark 2:18), and departing from the common translation "wedding guests" (as in the RSVCE).

an important part of Jewish practice: See Noah Hacham, "Fasting," in Collins and Harlow, eds., *The Eerdmans Dictionary of Early Judaism*, 634–36.

85 **"Can the sons of the bridechamber fast":** RSVCE, slightly adapted.

86 **familiarity with ancient Jewish practice and belief:** See especially Klyne R. Snodgrass, *Stories with Intent: A Comprehensive Guide to the Parables of Jesus* (Grand Rapids, Mich.: Eerdmans, 2008), 1–31. See also Arland J. Hultgren, *The Parables of Jesus: A Commentary* (Grand Rapids, Mich.: Eerdmans, 2000), 332–41; Brad H. Young, *Jesus and His Jewish Parables: Rediscovering the Roots of Jesus' Teaching* (New York: Paulist, 1989).

In order to grasp the meaning: Hultgren, *The Parables of Jesus*, 2.

87 **"After this Pharaoh gave a marriage feast":** This translation is from Charlesworth, ed., *The Old Testament Pseudepigrapha*.

"The point of the comparison": Adela Yarbro Collins, *Mark: A Commentary*, Hermeneia: A Critical and Historical Commentary on the Bible (Minneapolis: Fortress, 2007), 198–99.

88 **Jesus refers to his disciples:** See Craig S. Keener, *A Commentary on the Gospel of Matthew* (Grand Rapids, Mich.: Eerdmans, 1999), 299–300; Davies and Allison, *The Gospel according to Saint Matthew*, 2:109.

88 **Jews were supposed to tie small straps:** See David Rothstein, "Phylacteries," in Collins and Harlow, eds., *The Eerdmans Dictionary of Early
Judaism,* 1086–88.

"Our Rabbis have taught": *Soncino Talmud,* slightly adapted. For the
sake of clarity, I have translated "shoshbin" in the singular, since there is
no English equivalent for "best men and best women." See also Tosefta
Berakoth 1:3: "Bridegrooms and all those engaged in [the performance
of] commandments are exempt from reciting the *shema'* and the Prayer,
as Scripture states, 'When you sit in your house'; this excludes those
who are engaged in [fulfilling] commandments; and 'when you walk by
the way' (Deuteronomy 6:7); this excludes bridegrooms." *The Tosefta,*
trans. Jacob Neusner, 2 vols. (Peabody, Mass.: Hendrickson, 2002).

89 **"the friends of the bridegroom who prepared":** See Isidore Epstein,
Sukkah (London: Soncino Talmud, 1984), loc. cit. Contrast Yarbro Collins, *Mark,* 198, who suggests that "sons of the bridechamber" can mean
either "wedding guests" or "groomsmen."

91 **the climax of the wedding was the night:** See "Home and Family,"
in *The Jewish People in the First Century: Historical Geography, Political History, Social, Cultural and Religious Life and Institutions,* ed. S. Safrai and M.
Stern, 2 vols. (Assen, The Netherlands: Van Gorcum, 1976), 2:757–60;
Adolf Büchler, "The Induction of the Bride and the Bridegroom into
the *huppah* in the First and the Second Centuries in Palestine," in *Livre
d'hommage à la mémoire du Dr. Samuel Poznanski* (Warsaw: Harrassowitz,
1927), 82–132.

separated from his groomsmen: "Our text thus distinguishes two pe-
riods: the period of joy, when the bridegroom was with the wedding
guests, and the period of mourning, when he will be absent" (Ulrich
Luz, *The Gospel of Matthew,* 3 vols., Hermeneia [Minneapolis: Fortress,
2001, 2005, 2007], 2:37).

"Jesus is the groom of God's people": Keener, *Commentary on the
Gospel of Matthew,* 300. See also Joel Marcus, *Mark,* 2 vols. Anchor Bible
27 and 27A (New York: Doubleday, 2000; New Haven, Conn.: Yale
University Press, 2009), 237.

92 **the symbolism of the bridechamber:** On the *huppah,* see Büchler,
"The Induction of the Bride and the Bridegroom into the *huppah,*"
82–132.

93 **it is customary for young couples:** Raphael Posner, "Marriage," in

Encyclopedia Judaica, ed. Cecil Roth, 18 vols. (Jerusalem: Keter, 1971), 11:1040–41.

"Like a bridegroom Christ went forth": See J. P. Migne, *Patrologia Latina* 39 (cols. 1986–87). I am grateful to Father Nile Gross for allowing me to adapt his translation of this text.

94 **"implies that the presence of Jesus":** Collins, *Mark,* 199.

"The clearest example of Jesus' use": Sigurd Grindheim, *God's Equal: What Can We Know About Jesus' Self-Understanding in the Synoptic Gospels?* Library of New Testament Studies 446 (London: T. & T. Clark, 2011), 127. See also R. T. France, *The Gospel of Mark,* New International Greek Testament Commentary (Grand Rapids, Mich.: Eerdmans, 2002), 139; J. C. O'Neill, "The Sources of the Parables of the Bridegroom and the Wicked Husbandmen," *Journal of Theological Studies* 39 (1988): 485–89.

"Jesus identifies himself here": Ratzinger, *Jesus of Nazareth,* 1:252.

95 **three aspects of Roman crucifixion:** On crucifixion in ancient Judaism, the definitive work for some time to come will be David W. Chapman, *Ancient Jewish and Christian Perceptions of Crucifixion,* Wissenschaftliche Untersuchungen zum Neuen Testament 2.244 (Tübingen, Germany: Mohr Siebeck, 2008; Grand Rapids, Mich.: Baker Academic, 2010). See also Michael O. Wise, "Crucifixion," in Collins and Harlow, eds., *The Eerdmans Dictionary of Early Judaism,* 500–501; Raymond E. Brown, *The Death of the Messiah: From Gethsemane to the Grave: A Commentary on the Passion Narratives in the Four Gospels,* 2 vols., Anchor Bible Reference Library (New York: Doubleday, 1994), 2:945–52; Joseph Zias and James H. Charlesworth, "Crucifixion: Archaeology, Jesus, and the Dead Sea Scrolls," in *Jesus and the Dead Sea Scrolls,* ed. James H. Charlesworth, Anchor Bible Reference Library (New York: Doubleday, 1992), 273–89; Martin Hengel, *Crucifixion in the Ancient World and the Folly of the Message of the Cross,* trans. John Bowden (Philadelphia: Fortress, 1977).

"the most wretched of deaths": Cited in Hengel, *Crucifixion,* 8.

"the most severe punishment": Hengel, *Crucifixion,* 59.

96 **prepared for the cross by scourging:** On the practice, see Keener, *The Gospel of John,* 2:1119; Brown, *The Death of the Messiah,* 1:851–52.

leather whips or thongs fitted with spikes: Keener, *The Gospel of John,* 2:1119.

[He] had them scourged: This translation, slightly adapted, is from *Josephus: The Jewish War Books III–IV,* trans. H. St. J. Thackeray, Loeb Classical Library No. 487 (Cambridge, Mass.: Harvard University Press, 1997); see Keener, *The Gospel of John,* 2:1119.

"the flogging . . . was a stereotyped part": Hengel, *Crucifixion,* 32.

forced to carry the beams of the cross: Keener, *The Gospel of John,* 2:1134.

97   **"Can anyone be found":** Cited in Hengel, *Crucifixion,* 30–31.

98   **"Whenever we crucify the guilty":** Cited in Hengel, *Crucifixion,* 50.

"the tree of shame": Cited in Hengel, *Crucifixion,* 44.

"extreme and ultimate penalty": Cited in Brown, *The Death of the Messiah,* 2:947; and Hengel, *Crucifixion,* 8.

"the slaves' punishment": Hengel, *Crucifixion,* 51.

99   **"I see crosses there":** Cited and translated in Hengel, *Crucifixion,* 25.

"Although some features of crucifixions": Keener, *The Gospel of John,* 2:1135.

normally crucified naked: See Keener, *The Gospel of John,* 2:1138 (with refs.); Brown, *The Death of the Messiah,* 1:870.

"A Roman citizen of no obscure": This translation is from *Dionysius of Halicarnassus: Roman Antiquities,* vol. 3, books 5–6.48, trans. Earnest Cary, Loeb Classical Library (Cambridge, Mass.: Harvard University Press, 1940). Cited in Brown, *The Death of the Messiah,* 1:870.

Even modern Western sensibilities about modesty: See Dionysius of Halicarnassus, *Roman Antiquities* 7.69.2; Artemidorus Daldianus, *Oneirokritika* 2.53; Valerius Maximus, *Facta* 1.7.4. Brown concludes that we cannot be sure whether Jesus was crucified with or without a loincloth (*The Death of the Messiah,* 2:952–53). He notes that there is conflicting patristic evidence, with some sources assuming Jesus was completely despoiled of his clothing (e.g., Melito of Sardis, *On the Pasch* 97), and others depicting him as retaining a loincloth (*Acts of Pilate* 10:1). Removing people's clothing before execution was not limited to crucifixion, but was so widespread that the ancient Jewish rabbis debated whether or not men (and even women) should be put to death with or without clothing. See Mishnah *Sanhedrin* 6:3: "When he was four cubits from the place of stoning they stripped off his clothes. A man is kept covered in front and a woman both in front and behind. So Rabbi Judah. But the Sages say: A man is stoned naked but a woman is not stoned naked."

100 **"When they [the Jewish fighters]"**: Cited and translated in Hengel, *Crucifixion*, 25–26. For other mass crucifixions in Judea, see Josephus, *War* 2:75; and *Antiquities* 17:295.

103 **"the crown is part of royal mockery"**: Brown, *The Death of the Messiah*, 1:866.

a crown on his wedding day: See Safrai, "Home and Family," in Safrai and Stern, eds., *The Jewish People in the First Century*, 758n2; Philip and Hanna Goodman, "Jewish Marriages Throughout the Ages," in *The Jewish Marriage Anthology* (Philadelphia: The Jewish Publication Society of America, 1965), 73; David Mace, "Marriage Customs and Ceremonies," in *Hebrew Marriage: A Sociological Study* (London: Epworth, 1953), 179, 182. Cited in Fehribach, *Women in the Life of the Bridegroom*, 123n26.

104 **"king for a day"**: Satlow, *Jewish Marriage in Antiquity*, 172.

he too is dressed like a king: Fehribach, *Women in the Life of the Bridegroom*, 123.

105 **the act of casting lots for Jesus' "tunic"**: Brown, *The Death of the Messiah*, 2:955.

106 **strikingly evocative of the "tunic"**: See Brown, *The Death of the Messiah*, 2:956–57.

"This vesture [of the high priest]": This translation is from *The Works of Josephus*, trans. William Whiston (Peabody, Mass.: Hendrickson, 1987).

John is highlighting the seemingly minor detail: See John Paul Heil, "Jesus as the Unique High Priest in the Gospel of John," *Catholic Biblical Quarterly* 57 (1995): 729–45; André Feuillet, *The Priesthood of Christ and His Ministers* (New York: Doubleday, 1975), 47; C. K. Barrett, *The Gospel According to St. John* (London: SPCK, 1967), 457.

107 **"For some, Jesus' seamless tunic"**: Feuillet, *The Priesthood of Christ and His Ministers*, 47.

"I will greatly rejoice in the LORD": Oswalt, *The Book of Isaiah*, 2:570n41. See also Grindheim, *God's Equal*, 126n4; Fitzmyer, *The Gospel According to Luke*, 2:599.

"Jerusalem said, I will greatly rejoice": Slightly adapted from Bruce D. Chilton, *The Isaiah Targum: Introduction, Translation, Apparatus and Notes*, Aramaic Bible 11 (Collegeville, Minn.: Liturgical Press, 1987), 119.

dressing in the white priestly garment: See Kaufman, *Love, Marriage, and Family in Jewish Law and Tradition*, 161–62; "Kitel," in Roth, ed., *Encyclopedia Judaica*, 10:1079. Intriguingly, Roth notes: "The day of marriage is considered a day of atonement for the groom and the bride, and the idea of atonement and penitence is also associated with that of death." For white garments worn on solemn occasions, see Jerusalem Talmud, *Rosh Hashanah* 1:3.

110   By smashing the legs: See Keener, *The Gospel of John*, 2:1150–51.

God took one of Adam's "sides": Victor P. Hamilton, *The Book of Genesis*, New International Commentary on the Old Testament (Grand Rapids, Mich.: Eerdmans, 1990), 1:179.

creation of Eve and the crucifixion: See esp. Hoskyns, *The Fourth Gospel*, 532–35; Edward Hoskyns, "Genesis I–III and St. John's Gospel," *Journal of Theological Studies* 21 (1919): 210–218. For a full discussion of the interpretation with arguments for and against, see Brown, *The Gospel According to John*, 2:946–952. On Jesus as the new Adam in John's Gospel, see Ronning, *The Jewish Targums and John's Logos Theology*, 84–115; Nicolas Wyatt, "Supposing Him to Be the Gardener (John 20:15): A Study of the Paradise Motif in John," *Zeitschrift für die Neutestamentliche Wissenschaft* 81 (1990): 24–38.

Adam falls into a deep sleep: The Greek Septuagint reads: "And he took one of his sides (*mian t‾on pleur‾on*)" (Genesis 2:21).

111   "[In] those two original humans": Cited in Elowsky, *John*, 2:328.

113   "In this double outpouring of blood": Ratzinger, *Jesus of Nazareth*, 2:226 (emphasis added).

5. The End of Time

117   "The groom would go out to receive the bride": Safrai, "Home and Family," in Safrai and Stern, eds., *The Jewish People in the First Century*, 758, citing Babylonian Talmud, *Berakoth* 59b.

"betrothed" for some time before they come to dwell: Cf. Luz, *The Gospel of Matthew*, 1:93–94

118   "[T]he wedding ceremony in the first century": Fehribach, *The Women in the Life of the Bridegroom*, 123.

allusion to the heavenly temple: See Keener, *The Gospel of John*, 2:932; Brown, *The Gospel According to John*, 2:618–20.

take his bride home with him: Compare Ronning, *The Jewish Targums and John's Logos Theology,* 154–55.

119   **Although there is much that could be said:** For in-depth studies, see especially Philip J. Long, *Jesus the Bridegroom:The Origin of the Eschatological Feast as a Wedding Banquet in the Synoptic Gospels* (Eugene: Pickwick, 2013); Snodgrass, *Parables with Intent,* 505–19; Marianne Blickenstaff, *"While the Bridegroom Is With Them": Marriage, Family, Gender, and Violence in the Gospel of Matthew,* Journal for the Study of the New Testament Supplement Series 292 (London: T. & T. Clark, 2005), 78–108; Luz, *The Gospel of Matthew,* 3:226–245.

      ancient Jewish weddings climaxed: See Luz, *Matthew,* 3:228n18.

120   **a proverbial image of the joyful climax:** Keener, *A Commentary on the Gospel of Matthew,* 596–97.

121   **the five wise virgins carry their lamps:** See Snodgrass, *Stories with Intent,* 511–18, for a similar explanation.

      "The bridegroom is Christ, the bride is the Church": *The Great Commentary of Cornelius A. Lapide: The Holy Gospel According to Saint Matthew,* vol. 2, trans. Thomas W. Mossman, rev. and completed by Michael J. Miller (Fitzwilliam, NH: Loreto, 2008), 469.

122   **"[Marriage] is also a symbol of a far greater mystery":** Scott Hahn, "The World as Wedding," in *Catholic for a Reason IV: Scripture and the Mystery of Marriage and Family Life* (Steubenville, Ohio: Emmaus Road, 2007), 10–11, citing de Vaux, *Ancient Israel,* 33–34: "She wore a veil (Ct 4:1, 3; 6:7) which she took off only in the bridal chamber," and Albrecht Oepke, *"apokalypsis,"* in *Theological Dictionary of the New Testament,* ed. Gerhard Kittel (repr., Grand Rapids, Mich.: Eerdmans, 1977), 3:556–71.

123   **Jesus will unveil the glory:** See D. A. McIlraith, *The Reciprocal Love Between Christ and the Church in the Apocalypse* (Rome: Pontifical Gregorian University, 1989), 94–10, 123–147, 170–204.

      when the angel shows the bride: On the bridal adornment, see David E. Aune, *Revelation,* 3 vols., Word Biblical Commentary 52C (Nashville: Thomas Nelson, 1998), 3:1121–22.

125   **First, the bride:** See Aune, *Revelation,* 3:1121–22.

      It is *Beulah* land: See Oswalt, *Isaiah,* 2:581.

126   **Second, the bride of the Lamb:** See Aune, *Revelation,* 3:1122.

      jewels symbolizing the twelve tribes: Aune, *Revelation,* 3:1165.

127 described as "foursquare," or a cube: See McKelvey, *The New Temple,* 167–76.

128 the bride of Jesus is depicted: See D. S. Russell, *The Method and Message of Jewish Apocalyptic: 200 B.C.–A.D. 200,* Old Testament Library (Philadelphia:Westminster, 1964), 280–84; David M. Russell, *The "New Heavens and New Earth": Hope for the Creation in Jewish Apocalyptic and the New Testament* (Philadelphia:Visionary, 1996).

129 look carefully at what Jesus had to say: For discussion, see Davies and Allison, *Saint Matthew,* 3:221–48; Marcus, *Mark,* 2:826–36; Fitzmyer, *The Gospel According to Luke,* 2:1298–1308.

130 the immortality of the soul after death: See George W. E. Nickelsburg, "Resurrection," in Collins and Harlow, eds., *The Eerdmans Dictionary of Early Judaism,* 1142–44; George W. E. Nickelsburg, *Resurrection, Immortality, and Eternal Life in Intertestamental Judaism and Early Christianity,* Harvard Theological Studies 56 (Cambridge, Mass.: Harvard University Press, 2006); N. T. Wright, *The Resurrection of the Son of God,* Christian Origins and the Question of God, vol. 3 (Minneapolis: Fortress, 2003), 129–200.

not believing in the bodily resurrection: See Günter Stemberger, "Sadducees," in Collins and Harlow, eds., *The Eerdmans Dictionary of Early Judaism,* 1179–81.

131 they will be immortal: Fitzmyer, *The Gospel According to Luke,* 2:1305.

132 Jesus' response to the Sadducees: See esp. Lucian Legrand, *The Biblical Doctrine of Virginity* (New York: Sheed and Ward, 1963), 71–80. Cf. Davies and Allison, *Saint Matthew,* 3:226–27.

"In the World to Come": Slightly adapted from *The Midrash on Psalms,* trans. William G. Braude, 2 vols. (New Haven:Yale University Press, 1959), 2:366–67.

133 Intriguingly, the rabbis even use: On the relationship between the rabbinic idea of the "world to come" and Jesus' teaching in the Gospels, see Dale C. Allison, Jr., *Constructing Jesus: Memory, Imagination, and History* (Grand Rapids: Baker Academic, 2010), 164–203.

134 required to abstain: See Legrand, *The Biblical Doctrine of Virginity,* 71–78.

6. The Bridal Mysteries

137 **the writings of the ancient Church Fathers:** For an excellent over-
view of patristic texts, see Chavasse, *The Bride of Christ,* 99–221.

139 **alluding to the ritual washing:** "[H]ere, the explicit mention of water
suggests not simply an extended metaphor for salvation, but a direct
reference to water baptism" (Andrew T. Lincoln, *Ephesians,* World Biblical Commentary 42, [Nashville: Nelson, 1990], 375).

"In both Jewish and Greek cultures": Peter S. Williamson, *Ephesians,*
Catholic Commentary on Sacred Scripture (Grand Rapids, Mich.:
Baker Academic, 2009), 166. For scholars who recognize the allusion to
the Jewish nuptial bath, see also James D. G. Dunn, *Baptism in the Holy
Spirit* (London: SCM, 1970): 162–63; R. P. Meyer, *Kirche und Mission in
Epheserbrief,* Stuttgarter Bibelstudien (Stuttgart: Katholisches Bibelwerk,
1977), 295, 298

an ordinary Jewish nuptial bath: Williamson, *Ephesians,* 166.

the bride was "made holy": Ilan, *Jewish Women in Greco-Roman Palestine,* 88–89.

140 **a mystery that flows from the passion:** Thomas Aquinas, chapter 5,
lecture 8, *Commentary on Saint Paul's Epistle to the Ephesians,* trans. Matthew Lamb, O.C.S.O. (London: Magi, 1966), 219.

"If Christ's death is the point in history:: Lincoln, *Ephesians,* 375.

the Church Fathers discussed: For example, the fourth-century
writer Didymus the Blind writes: "In the baptismal pool, he who made
our soul takes it for his Bride" (Didymus, *On the Trinity,* cited in Jean
Daniélou, *The Bible and the Liturgy* (Notre Dame: University of Notre
Dame Press, 1956), 192.

"When you hear the texts from Scriptures": All translations from
Cyril cited hereafter are from *The Works of Saint Cyril of Jerusalem,* trans.
Leo P. McCauley S.J. and Anthony A. Stephenson, 2 vols., The Fathers
of the Church 61 and 64 (Washington, D.C.: Catholic University of
America Press, 1969, 1970), 1:75–76.

141 **the practice of disrobing at baptism:** So also Gregory of Nyssa: "I
have put off my garment, how shall I put it on?" (Song 5:3) By this the
Bride promises not to put on again the garment which has been taken
off, but to content herself with only one garment, according to the
precept given by the disciples. This garment is that with which she was

clothed, in being renewed in Baptism." (Gregory of Nyssa, *Commentary on the Song of Songs,* 46.) Cited in Daniélou, *The Bible and the Liturgy,* 195.

"Immediately, then, upon entering": See McCauley and Stephenson, trans., *The Works of Saint Cyril of Jerusalem,* 1:161–62; cited in Daniélou, *The Bible and the Liturgy,* 195.

142   **"[The Lord] will pour upon you clean water":** McCauley and Stephenson, trans., *The Works of Cyril of Jerusalem,* 1:117–118; cited in Daniélou, *The Bible and the Liturgy,* 197.

"Baptism is seen in its fullness": Daniélou, *The Bible and the Liturgy,* 200.

143   *"The one who receives Baptism":* John Paul II, *Man and Woman He Created Them: A Theology of the Body,* trans. Michael Waldstein (Boston: Pauline, 2006), 482–83.

144   **"Baptism, the entry into the People of God":** It is worth noting that this paragraph is quoted by Pope Benedict XVI in his Post-Synodal Apostolic Exhortation Sacrament of Charity (*Sacramentum Caritatis*), February 22, 2007, no. 27.

145   **"Let us rejoice and exult":** RSVCE, slightly adapted.

the wedding supper described here: See Aune, *Revelation,* 3:1029–30.

146   *"The eucharistic connotation":* Roch A. Kereszty *Wedding Feast of the Lamb: Eucharistic Theology from a Historical, Biblical, and Systematic Perspective* (Chicago: Hillenbrand Books, 2004), 80. See also Michael Barber, *Coming Soon: Unlocking the Book of Revelation and Applying Its Lessons Today* (Steubenville, Ohio: Emmaus Road, 2005), 230.

"Every Celebration [of the Eucharist]": Cited in Chavasse, *The Bride of Christ,* 147–48.

147   **"You have come to the altar":** Cited in Daniélou, *The Bible and the Liturgy,* 205. See also Roy J. Deferrari, *Saint Ambrose: Theological and Dogmatic Works,* The Fathers of the Church, vol. 44 (Washington, D.C.: Catholic University of America Press, 1963), 311.

"the kiss given by Christ to the soul": Daniélou, *The Bible and the Liturgy,* 205.

148   **"O Son of God, bring me into communion":** The Divine Liturgy of St. John Chrysostom; cited in the *Catechism of the Catholic Church,* no. 1386.

149   **this kind of self-gift:** See Brant Pitre, *Jesus and the Jewish Roots of*

the Eucharist: Unlocking the Secrets of the Last Supper (New York: Image, 2011).

150 **sacrificial love for the Church:** See Chavasse, *The Bride of Christ,* 109.

151 **Be subject to one another:** RSVCE, slightly adapted.

152 **all the issues raised:** For discussion, see Williamson, *Ephesians,* 154–78; and John Paul II, *Man and Woman He Created Them,* 465–90.

Paul uses the exact same Greek word: Williamson, *Ephesians,* 163.

153 **possess** *equal dignity:* Williamson, *Ephesians,* 160.

the author [of Ephesians]: John Paul II, *Man and Woman He Created Them: A Theology of the Body,* trans. Michael Waldstein (Boston: Pauline, 2006), 473.

the relationship between Christ and the Church: Lincoln, *Ephesians,* 381.

155 **Saint Paul's insight into the mystery:** See *St. John Chrysostom on Marriage and Family Life,* trans. Catherine P. Roth and David Anderson, Popular Patristics Series 7 (Crestwood, NY: St. Vladimir's Seminary Press, 1986).

Pay attention to love's high standard: Cited in Mark J. Edwards, *Galatians, Ephesians, Philippians,* Ancient Christian Commentary on Scripture, New Testament VIII (Downers Grove, Ill.: InterVarsity Press, 1999), 195.

156 **when the Christian wife supports her husband:** See John Chrysostom, *Homily on Ephesians* 20:5:33; cited in Edwards, *Galatians, Ephesians, Philippians,* 200.

"Tell her that you love her": Roth and Anderson, trans., *St. John Chrysostom on Marriage and Family Life,* 60–61.

spouses will be infinitely closer: In this regard, see the comments of Tertullian: "All the more we shall be bound to them [our departed spouses], because we are destined to a better estate, destined to rise to a spiritual partnership. We will recognize both our own selves and those to whom we belong. Else how shall we sing thanks to God to eternity, if there shall remain in us no sense and memory of this relationship? . . . Consequently, we who are together with God shall remain together. . . . In eternal life God will no more separate those whom he has joined together than in this life where he forbids them to be separated (Tertullian, *On Monogamy* 10; cited in Christopher A. Hall, *Mark,* Ancient Christian Commentary on Scripture, New Testament II [Downers Grove, Ill.: InterVarsity Press, 1998], 170).

157 **a few modern Church leaders:** See, for example, Leo XIII, Encyclical On Christian Marriage (*Arcanum*), February 10, 1880; Pius XI, Encyclical On Christian Marriage (*Casti Connubii*), December 31, 1930; Paul VI, Encyclical On Human Life (*Humanae Vitae*), July 25, 1968; John Paul II, Apostolic Exhortation on the Role of the Christian Family in the Modern World (*Familiaris Consortio*), November 22, 1981; Ramón García de Haro, *Marriage and the Family in the Documents of the Magisterium: A Course in the Theology of Marriage,* trans. William E. May (San Francisco: Ignatius, 1993).

158 **Christian marriage to be indissoluble:** See, for example, Curtis Mitch and Edward Sri, *The Gospel of Matthew,* Catholic Commentary on Sacred Scripture (Grand Rapids, Mich.: Baker Academic, 2010), 237–42; Luz, *Matthew,* 2:493–94; Angelo Cardinal Scola, *The Nuptial Mystery,* trans. Michelle K. Borras (Grand Rapids, Mich.: Eerdmans, 2005), 263–69; Alejandro Díez Macho, *Indisolubilidad del matrimonio y divorcio en la Biblia: La sexualidad en la Biblia* (Madrid: Fe Católica, 1978).

159 **the mystery of Christian virginity:** On consecrated virginity, see especially Pope John Paul II, post-synodal apostolic exhortation On the Consecrated Life (*Vita Consecrata*), March 25, 1996; Mary Jane Klimisch, OSB, *The One Bride: The Church and Consecrated Virginity* (New York: Sheed and Ward, 1965); Legrand, *The Biblical Doctrine of Virginity*; Pope Pius XII, encyclical On Consecrated Virginity (*Sacra Virginitas*), March 25, 1954.

161 **describe three categories of people:** For discussion, see Davies and Allison, *Saint Matthew,* 3:21–25.

"Like the miracles and the sacraments": Legrand, *The Biblical Doctrine of Virginity,* 443; for similar comments, see Pierre Grelot, *Man and Wife in Scripture,* trans. Rosaleen Brennan (New York: Herder and Herder, 1964), 93–94.

162 **"Virgins, persevere in what you have begun":** Cited in Arthur A. Just Jr., *Luke,* Ancient Christian Commentary on Scripture, New Testament III (Downers Grove, Ill.: InterVarsity Press, 2003), 313.

"She is a virgin who is the bride of God": This translation is from *Nicene and Post-Nicene Fathers, Second Series,* ed. Philip Schaff, et al., 14 vols. (repr., Peabody, Mass.: Hendrickson, 1994), 10:371.

163 **"[Lord,] among your many gifts":** See *The Rites of the Catholic Church,* vol. 2 (Collegeville, Minn.: Liturgical Press, 1991), 168–170.

the fulfillment of the unbreakable covenant: Homily for Rite of Consecration to a Life of Virginity, in *The Rites of the Catholic Church, Volume Two,* 168–70.

164   the priest's gift of himself: See Pope John Paul II, Apostolic Letter On the Dignity and Vocation of Women (*Mulieris Dignitatem*), August 15, 1988, no. 26.

Appendix

169   many of these writings: These ancient Jewish writings are drawn on in different ways in the following recent major works on the historical Jesus: Dale C. Allison, Jr., *Constructing Jesus: Memory, Imagination, and History* (Grand Rapids, Mich.: Baker Academic, 2010); Maurice Casey, *Jesus of Nazareth: An Independent Historian's Account of His Life and Teaching* (London: T. & T. Clark, 2010); Craig S. Keener, *The Historical Jesus of the Gospels* (Grand Rapids, Mich.: Eerdmans, 2009); John P. Meier, *A Marginal Jew: Rethinking the Historical Jesus,* 4 vols., Anchor (Yale) Bible Reference Library (New York: Doubleday/New Haven, Conn.: Yale University Press, 1991, 1994, 2001, 2009); James D. G. Dunn, *Jesus Remembered,* Christianity in the Making, vol. 1 (Grand Rapids, Mich.: Eerdmans, 2003); Craig A. Evans, *Jesus and His Contemporaries: Contemporary Studies* (Leiden, The Netherlands: Brill, 1994).

ACKNOWLEDGMENTS

This study had its origin in a presentation given almost a decade ago. Since that time, I have been assisted by countless friends, family, and colleagues in transforming what was a short lecture into a full-length book. Special thanks goes to Gary Jansen, Carie Freimuth, and the entire team at Image Books their amazing help and (even more amazing) patience with me over the course of the very difficult time in which the book was being written. Words cannot express my gratitude to you all.

I'd also like to thank the seminarians and lay students at Notre Dame Seminary New Orleans who willingly subjected themselves to my elective course on "Jesus the Bridegroom" in Fall 2012. Your enthusiasm for the subject was contagious, and the insights you shared in the classroom deeply impacted the final shape of the book (though you'll get no footnotes from me!).

I'm also profoundly grateful to Fr. Josh Rodrigue and Fr. André Melancon for their hospitality in giving me a quiet (and spacious) place to write at the cathedral of St. Francis de Sales in Houma. My good friend Dr. Michael Barber gave me invaluable assistance in reading through the manuscript and preserving me from some (though probably not all!) of my habitual infelicities of thought and expression.

Last, but certainly not least, I must thank my wife, Elizabeth, and our children—Morgen, Aidan, Hannah, Marybeth, and Lillia—for putting up with yet another one of "Daddy's books." Thank you for sharing your precious lives with me in our jumbled little domestic participation in the "great mystery" (Ephesians 5:32).